Recipes From Wisconsin With Love

By

Laurie Gluesing

and

Debra Gluesing

Illustrated by
Alvera M. Lundin

ISBN: 0-913703-05-2

1st printing: May, 1984

Edited by Barbara Ladd
Gigi Lambrecht

Typesetting by Superior Graphics
Minneapolis, Minnesota

Printed by Banta Company
Menasha, Wisconsin

Published by New Boundary Designs, Inc.
1453 Park Road
Chanhassen, MN 55317

Ordering information for additional copies is located at the back of the book.

Cover Design: "From Wisconsin . . . With Love"

Recipes From Wisconsin With Love is our amalgamation of some of the favorite cooking of Wisconsin residents and a gallimaufry of Wisconsin folklore, history and pertinent (or, in some cases, impertinent) information.

We have made the acquaintance of some of Wisconsin's best cooks through their submitted recipes, which run the gamut from everyday to gourmet. The pleasure has been ours.

May the joy of good eating make these pages much spilled on. May the love of Wisconsin and its lore make them all dog-eared.

To Wisconsin with Love,

Laurie Gluesing

Debra Gluesing

CONTENTS

Breads and Breakfast

Recipes from Wisconsin with Love...

The first church in Chilton was built by the women of the area. When the local men offered to put new siding on the church—if the women would quit holding temperance meetings—the women refused. Instead, they held bazaars and sold their baked goods, raising money to side the church themselves. Overnite rolls were probably a big success.

Overnight Rolls

"A wonderful make-ahead yeast dough"

1¼ **cups milk**
½ **cup shortening or butter**
2 **packages active dry yeast**
3 **eggs**
⅓ **cup sugar***
1 **teaspoon salt**
4½ **to 5 cups flour**

Scald milk. Add shortening or butter; stir until melted. Cool to lukewarm (115°). Sprinkle yeast over cooled milk mixture and let stand 10 minutes. Meanwhile, in large bowl, beat eggs. Gradually add sugar and salt. Blend yeast into milk; add to beaten eggs and stir well. At medium speed, gradually add flour and beat several minutes (batter will resemble thick cookie dough). Turn dough into a large, greased container, cover tightly and refrigerate at least 8 hours or overnight. When ready to bake, remove dough from refrigerator and let stand 30 minutes; punch down. Shape as desired, placing onto greased baking sheet. Cover with damp towel and let rise until nearly doubled (about 2 hours). Bake in preheated 425° oven for 12 to 15 minutes.**

*For sweet rolls double amount of sugar.

**Dough may be refrigerated several days, allowing you to use just the amount you want during that time. However, dough must be punched down occasionally, or weighed with a plate to keep from rising.

Makes 3 dozen

It never hurts to have a short-cut. If you don't need to knead, try this bread from frozen bread dough. It's delicious!

Cheese-Onion Loaf

1 loaf frozen bread dough, thawed
1½ cups grated sharp Cheddar cheese
½ cup finely minced onion
Paprika

Roll dough on lightly greased or flour surface to a rectangle about 10 x 18-inches. Sprinkle with cheese and onion. Roll, beginning at a long end, jelly roll style. Place on greased baking sheet, seam side down. Curve loaf into semi-circle and makes slashes a half-inch deep about one inch apart across the top of the loaf. Cover with a damp towel and let rise until double. Sprinkle with paprika and bake in a preheated 350° oven 25 to 30 minutes or until loaf sounds hollow when tapped on top.

Makes 1 loaf

Recipes from Wisconsin with Love...

Wisconsin played host to many gangsters from Chicago. Back in the 1930's the famous gangster, John Dillinger, hid out at Little Bohemia, a resort near Manitowish. A shoot-out with the Feds in 1934 forced Dillinger and his gang to flee.

Dill Bread
"Dill-icious"

1 package active dry yeast
¼ cup warm water
1 cup creamy cottage cheese
2 tablespoons sugar
1 tablespoon dried minced onion
1 tablespoon melted butter
2 teaspoons dill
1 teaspoon salt
¼ teaspoon baking soda
1 egg
2¼ to 2½ cups flour

Dissolve yeast in warm (110°) water; set aside. Combine cottage cheese, sugar, onion, melted butter, dill, salt, baking soda, egg; blend well. Stir in yeast. Add flour, a half cup at a time, beating well after each addition.

Cover with a damp towel or plastic wrap and let rise until nearly doubled. Stir dough down with a spoon. Turn into a greased 8-inch round 1½ or 2-quart casserole. Cover with damp towel or plastic wrap and let rise again until nearly doubled. Bake in a preheated 350° oven 40 to 50 minutes, until golden brown. If desired, brush with butter and sprinkle with coarse salt just after removing from oven.

Makes 1 round loaf

Recipes from Wisconsin with Love...

The Flavor of Wisconsin, a cookbook by Harva Hachten, is "about those who came to Wisconsin, and particularly about the ways they laid their tables." Most of the recipes in this book were selected from the entries in the "heritage cookbook contest" sponsored by the State Historical Society of Wisconsin and their extensive archives were the source of the historical information. The following Fry Bread recipe is reprinted from *The Flavor of Wisconsin* with our appreciation.

Indian Fry Bread
"Dough Gods"

12 cups flour
 3 cups lukewarm water
¼ to ½ teaspoon salt
 3 teaspoons baking
    powder
    Shortening for frying

Put flour into a 6-quart bowl and push up high along the sides so there is a deep well in the center. Add water combined with salt and baking powder, pouring it into the prepared well. Mix with a spoon until the dough will not absorb any more flour. Knead well in the bowl. Let stand 1 hour. Heat shortening in a large frying pan until very hot, but not smoking. With a knife, cut a piece of dough about the size of a small fist, and with floured hands, stretch it out flat. Drop into hot shortening. Brown both sides, turning once.

Recipes from Wisconsin with Love . . .

Johnny cakes were originally called "journey cakes" because they could easily be carried on journeys, and taste as good at the end of the trip as at the beginning. Simple and nutritious, this recipe was also standard fare in the logging camps of northern Wisconsin. The lumberjacks often ate them as individual cakes smothered with the locally produced maple syrup.

Johnny Cake

"Have cornbread will travel"

1 cup cornmeal	Sift together dry ingredients. In separate bowl, beat together egg, melted lard and sour milk. Combine liquid and dry ingredients with a few rapid strokes. Turn into greased cast-iron skillet or 9 x 9-inch baking pan. If desired, sprinkle top of batter with a few extra tablespoons sugar. Bake in 425° oven 20 minutes or until done.

1 cup cornmeal
¾ teaspoon salt
⅔ cup sugar
1½ cups flour
1 teaspoon baking soda
1 egg
2 to 3 tablespoons melted lard
1 to 1¼ cup sour milk *

Sift together dry ingredients. In separate bowl, beat together egg, melted lard and sour milk. Combine liquid and dry ingredients with a few rapid strokes. Turn into greased cast-iron skillet or 9 x 9-inch baking pan. If desired, sprinkle top of batter with a few extra tablespoons sugar. Bake in 425° oven 20 minutes or until done.

*If necessary, stir 1 teaspoon vinegar or 2 teaspoons lemon juice into milk to sour.

Makes a 9 x 9-inch pan

Recipes from Wisconsin with Love...

Scandinavians used to make lefse to use potatoes from the root cellar before they sprouted. Now, either fresh potatoes are used, or as in this recipe, instant potatoes. While there are as many lefse recipes as there are lefse makers, good lefse also requires a touch of magic. Here is a simple and good recipe. You supply the magic!

Lefse
"Basic and fool-proof"

3   cups water
½   cup butter or margarine
3   cups instant potato
      flakes
1   cup instant Carnation
      milk™
2   teaspoons sugar
1½ teaspoons salt
1½ cups flour

Bring water to boil; add butter or margarine and stir until melted. Add instant potato flakes, instant milk, sugar and salt, stirring to blend. Remove from heat and cool thoroughly in refrigerator. Remove dough from refrigerator and work in flour. Turn onto lightly floured surface and knead until dough is no longer sticky. Divide dough into golf ball-sized parts and roll each into very thin rounds, turning dough often while rolling for even thickness. Preheat ungreased lefse griddle to medium heat (about 300°). One at a time, bake lefse on one side until top bubbles slightly, turn carefully to other side and bake until underside is slightly dappled brown. Remove to damp towel covered with waxed paper; place a sheet of waxed paper over each lefse as it is brought to the pile and cover stack with another damp towel. Lefse may be eaten immediately or frozen until ready to use.

Makes about 25

Recipes from Wisconsin with Love...

"Shake Rag Under the Hill" is the famous street in the Pendarvis restoration at Mineral Point in southwestern Wisconsin. This is where most of the Cornish lead miners built their stone and log homes, down the hill from the mines. Their wives would signal mealtime to them by shaking their dishrags out of their doors, thus giving the street its name. Good Cornish wives served Saffron Bread often.

Saffron Bread

"Cornish Shake Rag bread"

3 cups boiling water
1 cup dried currants
1 cup raisins
1 teaspoon ground saffron
2 cups flour
2 teaspoons baking powder
½ teaspoon nutmeg
½ cup butter or margarine
1 cup sugar
2 eggs
1 teaspoon lemon extract flavoring

Pour two cups boiling water over currants and raisins; soak 15 minutes and drain. Pour remaining cup of boiling water over saffron and allow to steep until thoroughly cooled. Combine flour, baking powder and nutmeg, stirring to blend well. Cream together butter and sugar; add eggs, one at a time, beating well after each addition. Stir in lemon extract. Add dry ingredients alternately with cooled saffron liquid, beating just until blended after each addition. Stir in raisins and currants. Pour into a greased and lightly floured loaf pan and bake in a 350° oven 45 minutes. Invert from pan to cool.

Makes 1 loaf

Wisconsin is a great apple producing state. The major apple growing areas are the coulee country around Gays Mills, the Bayfield area and west central Wisconsin. Of the 100 varieties grown in Wisconsin, national favorites are the Jonathan, Golden Delicious and McIntosh. The McIntosh is an excellent apple for making applesauce because of its juicy pulp and rich tart taste.

Applesauce Puffs

2 cups commercial biscuit mix
¼ cup sugar
1 teaspoon cinnamon
¼ cup milk
1 egg
2 tablespoons vegetable oil
½ cup applesauce

Topping:
¼ cup sugar
¼ teaspoon cinnamon
3 tablespoons butter, melted

Sift together dry ingredients in large bowl; set aside. Beat together milk, egg and oil; add applesauce and stir until well blended. Combine liquid and dry ingredients with a few swift strokes. Fill well-greased muffin cups about two-thirds full and bake in preheated 400° oven 15 minutes. Meanwhile, place melted butter in one small bowl and combine sugar and cinnamon in another. When muffins are just out of oven, remove each from its cup, dip top in butter and then in sugar and cinnamon.

Makes 1 dozen

Recipes from Wisconsin with Love...

Walking on the ice one winter day, a visitor to Wisconsin met a man sawing ice for his icebox. The visitor said, "Pretty cold day to be cutting ice, isn't it?" The Wisconsinite, pulling the saw back and forth, replied, "Not so bad for me, but kinda chilly for the guy on the other end!"

Refrigerator Bran Muffins

2 cups water
2 cups Nabisco 100% Bran cereal™
1 cup shortening
3 cups sugar
4 eggs
1 quart buttermilk
5 cups flour
5 teaspoons baking soda
1 teaspoon salt
4 cups Kellogg's All Bran cereal™

Bring water to boil and pour over 100% Bran; cool. In very large mixing bowl, cream together shortening, sugar and eggs. Add buttermilk to bran and stir. Sift together flour, baking soda and salt; add to creamed mixture alternately with bran mixture, beating well after each addition. Stir in All Bran™. Refrigerate in covered container up to six weeks, baking desired amount whenever needed. To bake, fill well-greased muffin cups about two-thirds full and place in preheated 375° oven for 20 to 25 minutes.

Makes about 8 dozen

Recipes from Wisconsin with Love...

From 1840 to 1880, Wisconsin was one of the major wheat producers in the United States. However, because of disease, pests, worn-out soil and competition from other areas, wheat production declined and was replaced by dairying.

Orange Wheat Germ Muffins

"A nutty taste"

1 **cup wheat germ**
1⅓ **cup flour**
¼ **cup sugar**
3 **teaspoons baking powder**
½ **teaspoon salt**
1 **teaspoon grated orange peel**
⅓ **cup oil**
1 **egg**
⅔ **cup orange juice**

Topping:
2 **tablespoons wheat germ**
2 **tablespoons sugar**
¼ **teaspoon cinnamon**
1 **tablespoon butter or margarine, melted**

Sift together dry ingredients and orange peel; set aside. Beat together oil, egg and orange juice. Combine liquid and dry ingredients with a few swift strokes. Fill well-greased muffin cups about two-thirds full. Mix together topping ingredients and sprinkle over batter, pressing in lightly with a spoon. Bake in preheated 400° oven for 18 to 20 minutes.

Makes 1 dozen

If you don't mind swatting mosquitoes, berry picking is a great way to spend a summer day in Wisconsin. The variety is great, and the fruits of your labor will be most satisfying.

Blueberry Muffins

2 cups flour
⅓ cup sugar
½ teaspoon salt
1 tablespoon baking powder
1 cup milk
¼ cup shortening, melted
1 egg
2 teaspoons lemon juice
¾ cup fresh blueberries*

Sift together dry ingredients in large bowl; set aside. Beat together milk, melted shortening, egg and lemon juice. Combine liquid and dry ingredients with a few swift strokes. Carefully fold in drained blueberries. Fill well-greased muffin cups about two-thirds full. Bake in pre-heated 400° oven for 20-25 minutes.

*Huckleberries can be used instead of, or in combination with, blueberries, even though they are not as sweet as the commercially-grown varieties.

Makes 1 dozen

Blueberry

Zucchini Bread
"Moist and cake-like"

2 cups grated zucchini
3 eggs
2 cups sugar
1 cup vegetable oil
3 cups flour
1 teaspoon salt
1 teaspoon baking soda
¼ teaspoon baking powder
2 teaspoons cinnamon
1 teaspoon nutmeg
2 teaspoons vanilla*
½ cup chopped walnuts*

Grate zucchini and drain excess liquid. Beat eggs lightly. Add sugar, oil and zucchini. Combine dry ingredients and add to egg mixture, beating until smooth. If desired, add vanilla and nuts. Pour batter into two greased loaf pans. Bake in a preheated 350° oven 1 hour.

*Optional

Makes 2 loaves

Recipes from Wisconsin with Love...

Wisconsin is famous for its beer and breweries. Although a glass of cold beer is unequaled for thirst quenching, beer also has nutritional value and can add flavor to everyday cooking. Try it in bread!

Beer Bread
"Real simple"

3 **cups self-rising flour**
1 **teaspoon baking powder**
2 **tablespoons sugar**
1 **12-ounce can warm beer**

Mix together flour, baking powder and sugar. Stir in beer. Pour into a greased loaf pan. Bake in a preheated 375° oven for 45 minutes.

Makes 1 loaf

Recipes from Wisconsin with Love...

For a breathtaking springtime outing, take a drive through one of the apple-producing areas to see and smell the orchards in bloom. In the fall, return to enjoy the harvest at one of the pick-your-own apple farms.

Apple Bread
"A breath of fresh air"

½ **cup shortening**
¾ **cup sugar**
2 **eggs**
2 **tablespoons sour milk***
1 **teaspoon vanilla**
1 **teaspoon baking soda**
½ **teaspoon salt**
2 **cups flour**
2 **cups pared and chopped apples**
½ **cup chopped walnuts**

Cream together shortening and sugar; add eggs, beating well. Stir in sour milk and vanilla. Combine baking soda, salt and flour; add gradually to egg mixture, beating well. Fold in apples and walnuts. Pour batter into a greased loaf pan. If desired, sprinkle top with a blend of cinnamon and sugar. Bake in a preheated 325° oven 50 to 55 minutes.

*If necessary, stir ¼ teaspoon vinegar into milk to sour.

Makes 1 loaf

Near Mayville is the Horicon National Wildlife Refuge. Anyone lucky enough to be in the area in the fall is treated to the memorable spectacle of thousands of Canadian geese blanketing the grounds. This is a major stopover point for the birds on their annual migration south.

Wild Goose Chase Crumb Cake
"Old-fashioned"

½ **cup margarine or vegetable shortening**
1 **cup firmly packed brown sugar**
1 **cup sugar**
2 **cups flour**
1 **teaspoon salt**
1 **teaspoon cinnamon**
½ **teaspoon ground cloves**
2 **eggs**
1 **cup buttermilk**
1 **teaspoon baking soda**
1 **tablespoon flour**

Cream together margarine and sugars. Sift together flour, salt and spices; cut into creamed mixture until crumbly and well mixed. Set aside 1 cup of this mixture for topping. Beat eggs and buttermilk together. Blend soda and 1 tablespoon flour together and stir into egg mixture; beat well. Stir into remaining crumb mixture until moistened. Pour into a greased 9 x 13-inch baking pan. Sprinkle reserved crumb mixture over the top. Bake in a preheated 350° oven for 25 to 30 minutes or until tested done.

Makes a 9 x 13-inch cake

In southwestern Wisconsin, along the Mississippi River, are steep-sided valleys with winding streams and rivers. These valleys, known as coulees, were untouched by the glaciers. Coulee Country is known for its apples, cheese and tobacco as well as for its rugged beauty.

Coulee Kuchen

"An apple delight"

½ cup butter or margarine
¾ cup sugar
1 egg
½ cup milk
¼ teaspoon lemon juice
1½ cups flour
2 teaspoons baking powder
½ teaspoon salt
3 or 4 apples, pared halved and thinly sliced

Topping:
¾ cup sugar
1 teaspoon cinnamon
¼ teaspoon nutmeg
2 tablespoons flour

Cream together butter and sugar; add egg and beat well. Stir in milk and lemon juice. Combine flour, baking powder and salt; add to creamed mixture and blend well. Spread batter over bottom of a greased 9 x 13-inch baking pan. Arrange apple slices on top. Combine topping ingredients and sprinkle over apples. Bake in a preheated 350° oven for 40 to 45 minutes.

Makes a 9 x 13-inch cake

Auntie's Coffee Cake

"Worth the work"

1 cup milk
2 packages active dry yeast
½ cup sugar
½ teaspoon salt
2 eggs
1 teaspoon almond flavoring
½ cup vegetable oil
4 cups flour
2 tablespoons butter or margarine, melted
½ cup brown sugar
1½ teaspoons cinnamon

Scald milk; cool to lukewarm (about 115°). Sprinkle yeast over milk and set aside 10 minutes. Stir in sugar and salt until dissolved. Beat eggs and add to yeast mixture with oil and flavoring. Add flour, a cup at a time, stirring well after each addition. Turn into greased bowl and let rise until nearly doubled in bulk. Punch down and knead lightly on floured surface. Divide dough in half. To shape, roll each half into a rectangle, approximately 9 x 15 inches; brush with melted butter and sprinkle with sugar and cinnamon mixture. Beginning on a long side, roll dough up and pinch seam to seal. On a greased cookie sheet, place dough, seam side down and shape into a ring, pinching to seal the edges. Make shallow slits on the top of each ring at ¾-inch intervals (wider, if desired). Cover with damp towel and let rise until nearly doubled. Bake in preheated 350° oven for 20 to 30 minutes.

Makes 2 rings

Recipes from Wisconsin with Love...

In the true Wisconsin spirit "the coffee pot is always on." But don't serve your coffee alone when the delicious smell of this kaffee kuchen can fill the house almost magically.

Kaffee Kuchen

½ cup butter or margarine
1 cup sugar
2 egg yolks
1½ cups flour
2 teaspoons baking powder
½ teaspoon salt
½ cup milk
2 stiffly beaten egg whites

Topping:
⅓ cup flour
¼ cup brown sugar
2 tablespoons butter or margarine

Cream together butter and sugar; add egg yolks and beat well. Combine flour, baking powder and salt; add alternately with milk, beating well after each addition. Fold in stiffly beaten egg whites. Pour into greased 9 x 9-inch pan. For topping, combine flour and brown sugar; cut in butter until mixture resembles coarse meal. Sprinkle over batter. Bake in a preheated 350° oven 30 minutes. Serve warm.

Makes 9 x 9-inch cake

Danish Kringle Strips

1 cup milk
2 cakes yeast*
½ cup butter or margarine
½ cup sugar
2 eggs
½ teaspoon salt
2 cups flour
½ teaspoon almond or
  lemon extract flavoring
  or
1 teaspoon finely crushed
  cardemon
  Butter

Filling:
  1 cup butter or margarine
  ½ teaspoon salt
  2¼ cups firmly packed
    brown sugar
  ½ teaspoon cinnamon
  2 cups cooked dates,
    prunes or raisins
Topping:
  1 egg
  2 tablespoons milk
  Sugar
  Finely minced nuts

Dissolve yeast in cold milk (remember to follow directions for proofing active dry yeast if you are NOT using cake yeast). Cream together butter and sugar; add eggs, one at a time, beating well after each addition. Stir in yeast mixture. Combine flour and salt and add to creamed mixture with desired flavoring, beating well. Turn onto a lightly floured board and knead lightly. Roll into an 8 x 12-inch rectangle. Spread two-thirds of dough with butter; fold unbuttered third of dough to the center, then fold the remaining third over to center. Repeat rolling, buttering and folding steps twice more. Cover with damp towel and refrigerate at least 2 hours. Roll onto a slightly floured surface in a rectangle with a thickness of ⅜-inch. Cut into four lengthwise strips, spread filling in the center of each strip, fold edges over filling and seal seams. Place strips seam side down on greased baking sheets; cover with a damp towel and let rise 45 minutes. Brush with a wash made by beating 1 egg with 2 tablespoons milk. Sprinkle with sugar and finely minced nuts. Bake in a 350° oven 15-20 minutes.

To make filling, cream together butter, salt, sugar and cinnamon until smooth and fluffy. Fold in the cooked dates, prunes or raisins. (A half cup of almond paste can be added with the thick, cooked fruit, if desired.)

*2 packages active dry yeast can be substituted for cake yeast. To substitute, scald milk and cool to lukewarm (110°) before combining with yeast.

Makes 4 strips

The first U.S. Secretary of Agriculture, Jeremiah M. Rusk, was from a farm in Viroqua. A big man with a flowing beard, "Uncle Jerry" also served in the Civil War, in the U.S. Congress and as Governor of Wisconsin. Rusk County is named for him.

Cardemon Rusk

"A Danish toast — perfect with coffee"

1 cup shortening
1½ cups sugar
2 eggs
1 cup sour cream
1 teaspoon crushed cardemon or cardemon seed
¼ teaspoon salt
1 teaspoon baking soda
½ teaspoon almond flavoring
3 cups flour

Cream together shortening and sugar. Beat eggs and add to creamed mixture with sour cream and almond flavoring. Combine remaining ingredients and blend into creamed mixture; beat well (batter will be thick). Pour into a greased and floured 9 x 13-inch baking pan. Bake in preheated 350° oven 30 to 40 minutes. Cool. Cut rusks into three lengthwise strips; cut each strip into ½-inch slices. Toast slices on ungreased baking sheet in a 225° oven about 45 minutes, or until lightly browned.

Makes 78 pieces

Recipes from Wisconsin with Love...

One of the first and only colonies of Icelanders to settle in the U.S. came to Washington Island, at the tip of Door County, in 1870. Lured by the bountiful waters of Lake Michigan, these island fishermen were well-suited to their new home.

Icelandic Pancakes

1 **cup flour**
¼ **cup sugar**
¼ **teaspoon cinnamon**
½ **teaspoon salt**
3 **cups milk**
3 **eggs**

Combine flour, sugar, cinnamon and salt; add milk gradually and beat thoroughly. Beat eggs. Gradually add to batter and blend well. Pour ¼ cup batter per cake onto a medium hot griddle greased with a few drops of oil. When bubbles form on the top of each pancake, flip and cook a few more minutes. Serve immediately.

Serves 4-6

Recipes from Wisconsin with Love...

Marathon County grows 90% of the cultivated ginseng in this country. The more valuable wild ginseng also grows in Wisconsin, but can be harvested only with a license. Most of the ginseng is exported to Asia, where it commands a high price. Because of the human-like shape of the root, it is believed to be a source of health and strength. Often brewed in tea, ginseng is valued for its properties as a tonic, an aphrodisiac, and a general cure-all. But since the medicinal value of ginseng is not proven, Grandma recommends her pancakes for whatever ails you.

Grandma's Pancakes
"Good for whatever ails you"

½ package active dry yeast
2 tablespoons warm water
2 cups flour
1 tablespoon baking soda
1 tablespoon baking powder
1 tablespoon sugar
2 cups buttermilk
2 tablespoons vegetable or olive oil
3 eggs
½ cup heavy cream or half-and-half

Dissolve yeast in warm water and set aside. Sift together flour, soda, baking powder and sugar. Beat together the buttermilk, oil and eggs; stir into flour mixture. add yeast and beat well. Stir in cream and beat well again. (If mixture is too thick, add a tablespoon more cream.) Pour into a large jar and let rise in refrigerator overnight. Pour ⅓ to ½ cup batter per cake onto a medium hot griddle greased with a few drops of oil. When bubbles form on the top of each pancake, flip and cook a few more minutes. Store leftover batter in refrigerator, stirring batter down every few days.

Makes 1 quart batter

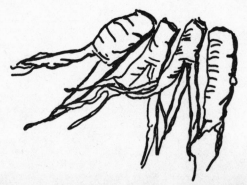

Mornings were cold in the logging camps of northern Wisconsin. One way the lumberjacks survived was to eat one pancake for each degree below zero. It was their eagerness for days of 40 below that helped give Wisconsin its reputation for cold winters.

Apple Pancakes
"Good in warm weather, too"

- **1** cup flour
- **2** teaspoons sugar
- **½** teaspoon salt
- **1½** cups milk
- **4** eggs
- **3** large sour apples
- **½** cup lemon juice

Sift together flour, sugar and salt; stir in milk, blending to make a smooth paste. Add eggs, one at a time, beating well after each addition. Pare and core apples, then cut in small, Julienne strips; marinate in lemon juice for several minutes. Drain apples and fold into batter. Pour ⅓ to ½-cup of batter per cake onto a medium hot griddle greased with a few drops of oil. When bubbles form on the top of each pancake, flip and cook a few more minutes. If desired, batter can be baked into one large pancake by pouring it into a greased, hot skillet and cooking until bubbles form; turn into a buttered baking dish, bubble-side-down and bake in preheated 350° oven until browned (about 7 minutes). Serve immediately with sweetened cream, sugar and cinnamon or syrup.

Serves 3 to 4

Recipes from Wisconsin with Love...

Zucchini Pancakes

3 **cups grated zucchini**
3 **eggs**
½ **cup flour**
¼ **cup vegetable oil**
1½ **teaspoons salt**

Drain zucchini on paper toweling to remove excess liquid. Beat eggs well; blend zucchini into eggs with oil and salt. Add flour and stir just until blended (batter will be slightly lumpy). Pour ¼-cup of batter per cake onto a medium hot griddle greased with a few drops of oil: tip skillet to spread batter thinly. When bubbles form on the top of each pancake, flip and cook a few more minutes. Serve immediately either with syrup or rolled up and topped with applesauce or yogurt.

Serves 4 to 6

Cheese Pancakes

1 **cup grated Swiss or Cheddar cheese**
⅔ **cup sour cream**
3 **egg yolks**
2½ **tablespoons flour**
1 **teaspoon grated lemon rind**
Dash of nutmeg
¼ **teaspoon salt**
⅛ **teaspoon pepper**

Combine cheese, sour cream, egg yolks and flour; beat well. Stir in lemon rind and seasonings. Drop 1 or 2 heaping tablespoons batter onto a hot, well-greased griddle; immediately reduce heat to low. Fry 4 or 5 minutes per side. Handle gently and keep warm until all are cooked.

Serves 4 to 6

German Oven Pancake

"Unbelievably good"

- **3** eggs
- **½** cup flour
- **½** teaspoon salt
- **½** cup milk
- **2** tablespoons vegetable oil
- **4** strips bacon

Beat eggs thoroughly. Gradually add flour and salt, beating well after each addition (batter should be smooth). Add milk and blend well. Stir in oil. Pour batter into a buttered, 10-inch skillet or a 9x9-inch baking pan; arrange bacon on top. Bake in a preheated 450° oven for 20 minutes, reduce oven to 350° and bake 10 minutes more. Serve immediately with syrup.

Serves 3 to 4

Recipes from Wisconsin with Love...

The early attempts of William Dempster Hoard to substitute dairy farming for the faltering wheat farms were not popular. In the 1860's there was scorn for any farmer who would be "tied to a cow." But by 1872, Hoard's personal forcefulness and his newspaper, "Hoard's Dairyman," initiated the founding of the Wisconsin Dairymen's Association. One of his favorite slogans was "Treat a cow as you would a lady."

Zucchini Quiche

4 eggs
1 cup commercial biscuit mix
½ cup vegetable oil
½ teaspoon salt
½ teaspoon marjoram
½ teaspoon chopped parsley
1 clove garlic, minced
1 small onion, chopped
3 cups thinly sliced zucchini
½ cup grated Cheddar cheese
½ cup grated Parmesan cheese

Beat eggs thoroughly. Blend in biscuit mix, oil, salt and herbs; beat well. Combine with remaining ingredients and pour into a greased 10-inch pie pan. Bake in a preheated 350° oven for 35 to 40 minutes. Cool at room temperature 10 minutes before serving.

Serves 4 to 6

Farmers began to follow Hoard's doctrines, adopting his slogan that the dairy cow is "the foster mother of the human race." Creameries, cheese factories and cheese shops sprang up everywhere in Wisconsin.

Spinach Vegetable Quiche
"Rather gourmet, but excellent"

3 tablespoons vegetable oil
¾ cup chopped green pepper
¾ cup chopped onion
1½ cups sliced mushrooms
1½ cups chopped zucchini
1½ teaspoons minced garlic
4 or 5 eggs
1 pound Ricotta cheese
1 teaspoon salt
⅛ teaspoon pepper
10 ounces frozen chopped spinach, thawed*
1 cup crumbled feta cheese or grated Cheddar cheese

In vegetable oil, sauté green pepper and onion just until hot; add mushrooms, zucchini and garlic and sauté just until tender. Do not overcook. Beat together eggs, Ricotta cheese, salt and pepper. Drain spinach thoroughly on paper toweling and add to egg mixture. Stir in sautéed vegetables. Mix the feta or Cheddar cheese and stir well to combine. Pour into a greased 10-inch quiche or pie pan and spread evenly. Bake in a preheated 350° oven 1 hour or until a knife inserted in center comes out clean. Cool at room temperature 10 minutes before serving.

*Fresh, sautéed spinach may be substituted.

8 Servings

Recipes from Wisconsin with Love . . .

Technology advanced with the rising importance of the dairy cow. The most valuable contribution was Babcock's Butterfat Tester, invented in 1890 by Stephan M. Babcock, a professor at the University of Wisconsin. His butterfat test made the farmers and creamery owners "more honest than the Ten Commandments ever did."

Bacon Quiche

6 or 7 slices bacon
1 medium onion, chopped
3 eggs
1 cup half-and-half
½ teaspoon salt
1 cup grated Swiss or Cheddar cheese
1 tablespoon flour
1 unbaked pastry shell for 9-inch pie

Fry or broil bacon until crisp; drain on paper toweling and crumble. Sauté onions in bacon drippings and drain. Beat together eggs and half-and-half. Stir in salt, crumbled bacon and onions. Toss together cheese and flour; arrange in bottom of pastry shell. Pour egg mixture over cheese and bake in a preheated 325° oven for 40 to 45 minutes, or until knife inserted in center comes out clean. Cool at room temperature 10 minutes before serving.

Serves 4 to 6

Many communities celebrate their heritage and promote their ethnicity through special events and programs. Among these are the Norwegian celebrations in Westby, Blue Mound and Mt. Horeb, and the Swiss festivities in Monroe and New Glarus. Traditional foods are one appealing way to retain links with the Old Country.

Swiss Cheese Pie

"A traditional recipe from the Old Country"

- 2 cups grated Swiss cheese
- 1 tablespoon flour
- 2 eggs
- 1½ cups half-and-half
- ½ teaspoon salt
- 1 medium onion, finely chopped
- 1 unbaked pastry shell for a 9-inch pie

Combine cheese, flour, eggs, half-and-half, salt and onion; mix well. Pour into the pastry shell and bake in a preheated 350° oven 50 minutes or until puffy and golden brown.

6 Servings

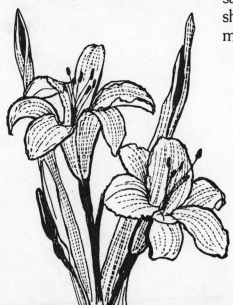

Crack of Dawn Breakfast

"Baked in a Pan"

½ cup butter or margarine
½ pound bacon, sausage or
   ham
2 cups grated Cheddar
   cheese

12 eggs
¼ to ½ teaspoon pepper
½ to 1 teaspoon salt
⅔ cup heavy cream

Spread butter in a 9x13-inch glass baking pan (the pan must be glass or Corningware™). Brown meat and arrange on bottom of pan; sprinkle with 1 cup of the cheese. Crack eggs over cheese, puncturing yolks with a tooth-pick. DO NOT STIR. Sprinkle with season-ings. Pour cream over egg mixture and top with remaining cheese. Cover and refrigerate overnight. Uncover and bake in a preheated 350° oven 30 to 45 minutes, depending on how hard the yolks are to be cooked.

8 Servings

Along the Wisconsin River the gillygaloo bird builds a square nest for its square eggs. This bird has never been seen, but it has often been heard saying "ouch" when laying its eggs. The lumberjacks used the eggs for dice to while away long evening hours.

Gillygaloo Omelette
"First find the square eggs"

¼ cup butter or margarine
18 eggs
1 cup sour cream
1 cup milk
2 to 3 tablespoons salt
¼ cup diced onion
½ cup diced ham or crumbled, fried bacon
2 tablespoons chopped green pepper
1 cup grated Cheddar or Swiss cheese

Melt butter in a 9x13-inch baking pan. Beat eggs and mix together with sour cream, milk and salt. Stir in onion, ham and green pepper. Pour over melted butter and bake in a preheated 350° oven 40 minutes. Sprinkle grated cheese over top of omelet and bake another 10 minutes. Cut into squares to serve.

12 Servings

Eggs in a Basket

6 commercial frozen puff
   pastry shells
6 eggs
6 slices Canadian bacon,
   fried
1 cup Hollandaise Sauce

Bake patty shells according to package directions, undercooking just slightly so tops are not browned. Cool. Remove the middle of each shell, being careful not to perforate the bottom or sides. Place on a baking sheet; crack an egg into the center of each shell. Bake in a 300° oven 40 to 45 minutes or until egg is set. Place each egg basket on a slice of fried Canadian bacon and pour Hollandaise sauce over all.

Easy Hollandaise Sauce:
3 egg yolks
1 tablespoon lemon juice
¼ teaspoon salt
⅛ teaspoon cayenne
½ cup butter, melted and
   very hot

To make Hollandaise, combine egg yolks, lemon juice, salt and cayenne in an electric blender; blend on low speed until yolks are lighter in color. With blender still beating at low speed, pour hot butter in a thin stream into the yolks. Continue blending until sauce is thick and smooth.

6 Servings

Recipes from Wisconsin with Love...

On a gala outing in 1825, two boatfuls of prominent Wisconsin citizens were rowing along the Green Bay shore. In the "yolking" spirit, they began throwing eggs at each other. The fun continued on shore until the ammunition was gone, leaving the beach covered with egg shells. Before leaving, members of the party made speeches to commemorate the battle, naming the site Egg Harbor.

Egg Harbor Omelette
"Toss eggs gently"

3 medium potatoes, pared and diced
¼ cup butter
⅓ cup finely chopped onion
1 cup diced cured ham
6 eggs
1 teaspoon salt
¼ teaspoon freshly ground pepper
2 tablespoons milk
1 tablespoon chopped parsley
½ cup finely chopped mushrooms
½ cup grated Swiss cheese

Cover potatoes with water in a saucepan, bring to a boil and cook 10 minutes or just until tender. Drain well. Melt butter in a large skillet, add onions and sauté until golden. Stir in potatoes and ham; cook 3 minutes. Beat eggs; stir in salt, pepper, milk and parsley. Pour into skillet over the potatoes and ham. Cook over high heat, stirring with a fork until eggs begin to thicken. Cook, without stirring, until the underside is browned. Sprinkle with mushrooms and cheese, place under a pre-heated broiler just until cheese melts and begins to bubble.

4 Servings

Recipes from Wisconsin with Love...

This farmer's breakfast recalls the hearty meals that were prepared in logging cook shanties and farm kitchens. The dish is great, but warrants a morning of hard work to wear it off!

Farmer's Breakfast

3 medium potatoes
1 tablespoon vegetable oil
1½ cups chopped ham
¼ cup finely chopped onion
1 tablespoon finely chopped green pepper
4 or 5 eggs
¼ to ½ teaspoon salt
dash of pepper *

Cook, peel and slice potatoes. Heat oil in large skillet. Over medium heat, brown potatoes, ham, onion and green pepper. Beat eggs and seasonings together; pour over browned vegetables. Stir constantly until eggs are cooked.

*Grated cheese can be added if desired.

3 to 4 Servings

Blueberry Syrup

1 cup fresh blueberries
½ cup unsweetened
   apple juice
1 teaspoon cornstarch
2 teaspoons water
½ teaspoon vanilla

Combine blueberries and apple juice; cook over medium heat until mixture begins to boil. Blend cornstarch and water; stir into blueberries. Boil 2 minutes, stirring constantly. Add vanilla. Cool slightly before serving over pancakes, waffles or French toast.

Makes 1 cup

Apple Butter

6 pounds apples
1 cup apple cider
2½ cups sugar
2 teaspoons cinnamon
1 teaspoon allspice
½ teaspoon cloves

Remove stems from apples. Place apples in a large kettle, cover with water and bring to a boil. Reduce heat and simmer until apples are tender. Drain. Puree through a food mill or sieve into a 3-quart saucepan. Discard seeds and skins. Add remaining ingredients to apple pulp; cook over low heat, stirring occasionally, until thickened. (This takes about 1½ hours.) Pour into pint canning jars to within ¼-inch of top. Seal and process in a boiling water bath canner for 10 minutes.

Makes 3 pints

Recipes from Wisconsin with Love...

One of the most natural of American experiences left in this highly commercialized world is to gather the sap from the rock, or sugar, maple in the spring and make it into syrup. Wisconsin, a large producer of pure maple syrup, affords the opportunity for this authentic experience. Very little has changed in the procedure since the days when the pioneers relied on maple syrup as a basic sweetener. It is still a festive occasion in many communities when friends and families gather to work together. It is strenuous work, but the thrill of tasting the "first run" is well worth it.

Holes are drilled in the trunk of the maple tree when snow is still on the ground and before the buds start to enlarge. A metal spout is hammered into the hole and a covered pail is hung from it. On the first days of thaw the sap slowly begins to drip, and the rounds of gathering the sap begin. A sledge drawn by horse or tractor holds a large tank into which the sap from each pail is poured. The sap is brought to the sugarhouse and emptied into a large pot. There it must be carefully tended over a low fire to keep the sap at a correct boil for inducing the best flavor as the long process of turning sap to syrup begins.

The yield from this lengthy procedure is small — one gallon of syrup from 30-40 gallons of sap. Many more days of boiling further reduces the syrup down to maple sugar. Maple syrup was strictly graded according to color until 1979, when the system was simplified to only two grades: Grade A (table quality), and Grade B (not table quality). Commercially packaged syrup has less than 5% pure maple syrup, so if this is the only form of syrup you've known, prepare for a marvelous surprise. Pure maple syrup is more subtle and delicate — the lighter the color the more delicate the flavor. Pure maple syrup can easily be substituted for molasses, brown sugar or cane sugar in many recipes. The best way to use it is all alone or in combination with mild ingredients. It blends well with apples, squash, sweet potatoes, peaches or pears.

Syrup Tips: 1) Refrigerate syrup after opening
2) If syrup crystallizes, heat jar without lid in hot water or microwave
3) If mold forms on syrup, skim it off top with a spoon and heat to 180°F. Then use as usual, since the mold is destroyed at this temperature.

Soups and Salads

Beets, carrots and potatoes are among the staples of Polish cooking. Obtainable even in lean years, these ingredients can be blended into an easy and tasty soup, Cold Borscht. The introduction of this dish into Wisconsin coincided with the immigration of large numbers of Eastern Europeans at the turn of the century, and the Poles are presently one of the largest ethnic groups in Wisconsin.

Borscht
"Cold beet soup"

1 **cup diced raw beets**
1 **cup diced carrots**
6 **cups water**
1 **cup diced potatoes**
½ **cup chopped onion**
1 **teaspoon salt**
½ **teaspoon pepper** *
1 **or 2 teaspoons sugar**

Garnish:
   Chopped cucumber or
   dill pickle
   Sour cream
   Hard boiled egg

Bring beets and carrots to boil in the water and cook 10 minutes. Add remaining ingredients; boil slowly for 10 to 15 minutes. Chill and serve with dollops of sour cream, chopped dill pickle, chopped cucumber and/or slices of hard boiled egg.

*May use 1 teaspoon peppercorns

Serves 6 to 8

Cucumber Soup
"Smooth and rich"

5   medium cucumbers
⅔   cup chopped onion
2   tablespoons butter or
    margarine
¼   cup flour
3   13½-ounce cans
    chicken broth
2   bay leaves
1   teaspoon salt
⅛   teaspoon white pepper
1   cup half-and-half
1   tablespoon lemon juice
1   tablespoon chopped
    fresh dill
½   cup sour cream*

Pare cucumbers. Thinly slice four cucumbers; cut remaining cucumber in half, remove seeds and chop. Melt butter in a large saucepan and sauté onion. Stir flour into onions all at once and continue stirring, over low heat, until flour expands. Gradually add broth to the cooked flour and onion, stirring constantly until thickened. Add all but 8 of the cucumber slices to the broth. Season with bay leaves, salt and pepper. Over medium heat, bring broth to a boil, reduce heat, cover and simmer 10 minutes. Remove bay leaves. Strain about two-thirds of the broth into a large saucepan and set aside. Purée the strained cucumbers and remaining broth in a blender; add to the strained broth. Stir in cream, lemon juice and the chopped, uncooked cucumber. Heat slowly to serving temperature. Or chill if desired. To serve, top each bowl of broth with a reserved cucumber slice, a dollop of sour cream and a sprinkling of dill.

*optional

Serves 6 to 8

Recipes from Wisconsin with Love...

Old World Wisconsin is history come to life. Located near Eagle, this vast outdoor living museum uses actual 19th century buildings to re-create the life and times of Wisconsin's pioneers. The scattered farm-steads and village reflect five different ethnic groups: Finns, Danes, Germans, Norwegians and Yankees. These settings help portray the varying cultures and traditions that these hardy settlers brought from their homeland to the New World.

Potato Cheese Soup

5 to 7 medium potatoes
4 to 6 tablespoons butter
  or margarine
1 medium onion, finely
  chopped
3 stalks celery, finely
  chopped
1 carrot, grated
3 or 4 tablespoons flour
2 cups milk
1 tablespoon parsley
6 to 8 slices cooked,
  crumbled bacon
2 or 3 teaspoons chicken
  bouillon
1 pound grated Cheddar
  cheese

Peel, dice and cook potatoes in lightly salted water until tender. Reserving water, drain potatoes and set half aside. Mash remainder of potatoes with a small amount of water. Melt butter in a large saucepan. Sauté onion, celery and carrot. Stir flour into sautéed vegetables all at once and continue stirring, over low heat, until flour expands. Gradually add milk, stirring constantly until thickened. Stir in mashed potatoes. Add reserved potatoes and water. Stir. Blend in remaining ingredients and heat, stirring constantly, until cheese is melted.

Serves 4

The first white person to see the area now known as Wisconsin was the French explorer, Jean Nicolet. Searching for the Northwest Passage, he landed at what is now Green Bay in 1634. Expecting to be greeted by Chinese, he dressed in a long flowing robe. Instead, he found a large settlement of Winnebago Indians.

French Onion Soup

"A little more gourmet"

1½   **pounds Spanish or yellow onions**
2   **tablespoons butter**
2   **tablespoons white wine**
6   **cups water**
6   **chicken bouillon cubes**
1   **bay leaf**
  Dash of thyme
  Dash of white pepper
8   **teaspoons cream**
  Seasoned croutons
8   **slices Swiss cheese**
2   **teaspoons grated Parmesan cheese**

Peel onions and slice thinly. Melt butter in frying pan. Sauté onions until tender—do not brown. Add wine, water and bouillon cubes; bring to a boil. Add bay leaf, thyme and white pepper; boil, uncovered, over high heat until liquid is reduced by one-third (about ½ hour). To serve, stir 1 teaspoon cream into each bowl of soup. Add four or five croutons, cover with a slice of Swiss cheese and sprinkle about ¼ teaspoon Parmesan cheese on top. Place each bowl under a broiler until cheese is browned.

Serves 8

Recipes from Wisconsin with Love...

France ruled the area which would later become Wisconsin for 129 years, until 1763. It was during these years that explorers and missionaries began to arrive, followed by fur traders and trappers.

French Onion Soup

"Country-style"

2 **large Spanish or yellow onions**
½ **cup butter**
4 **cups beef broth** *
   Dash of salt
   Dash of pepper
4 **slices plain or toasted French bread**
½ **cup Parmesan, Swiss or Cheddar cheese**

Peel onions and slice thinly. Melt butter in frying pan. Sauté onions until golden—do not brown. Add broth and simmer, covered, until onions are tender. Add pepper and salt, if needed. To serve, float a slice of bread on top of each bowl of broth; sprinkle with cheese and dot with butter. Bake, uncovered, until cheese is lightly browned and the bread is puffed.

*Consommé or bouillon can be used.

Serves 4

Stone Soup

1 smooth, rough, small,
  large or medium-sized
  stone
1 clever tramp
1 Kickapoo Valley town in
  the 1930s

During the 30's hard times were easy to come by. Drifters, floaters, tramps and gypsies traveled the length and breadth of the Kickapoo looking for hand-outs. Some were willing to trade an honest day's labor for the food which they sought. Others managed to hoard their strength, yet always find plenty to eat. These were the lucky ones who possessed the magical stones from which the heartiest, zestiest, most tasty soups ever known in the Kickapoo Valley could be made.

Records show that the first such stone and its owner visited Soldiers Grove on a hot, dry, dusty August evening in 1934. On that particular night a weary couple sat fanning themselves on their front porch, waiting for the sun to sink in the west and bring some relief from the heat. As the evening wore on a tramp approached their gate and asked if he might borrow a kettle. Now, the Kickapoo Valley in those days was not known for its generosity toward tramps and other hapless wanderers, but the couple saw no harm in lending an old kettle, especially when the fellow agreed to do his cooking right in their own back yard. They watched as the tramp lit a fire, filled the kettle full of water and put it on to boil. Their eyes opened wide as he plunked one small smooth stone into the kettle. He added nothing more and the wife wondered aloud as to what he was up to. "Why, mam," said the tramp, "the stone which you just saw me drop into your kettle is a real special one. It's magical. You wait and see. In an hour or so it will make the heartiest, zestiest, most tasty soup the Kickapoo Valley has ever known."

Recipes from Wisconsin with Love . . .

The couple just had to share this incredible news with the neighbors. Before long the party lines had done their work and a crowd began to gather around the tramp.

The minutes ticked by. Every so often the tramp would stir the contents and take a sip. "You know," he'd say, "this soup's coming right along."

"Here, let me have a taste," one of the on-lookers offered. As he sipped, the crowd waited . . . "Well, if you don't mind my saying so, I think your soup could use a little salt and pepper."

"Mighty kind of you to take an interest in my soup. You just go ahead and add whatever amount seems right." And he did.

The soup boiled on. "Would you like a taste," the tramp offered a lady nearby with upraised eyebrows.

"Not bad," she commented, "but an onion would liven things up."

"You're probably right. Add an onion if you'd like." And she did.

A few minutes more . . . another sip. "How about adding a little meat?" suggested the next taster.

"Good idea," replied the tramp and two fine lean hunks of beef were handed to the tramp which he cut into small chunks and dropped in the kettle.

"Would you consider adding some of my homemade noodles?" asked another lady.

"If you think it would improve things, why not?" said the tramp, and a pound of fresh noodles was added to the kettle.

Every on-looker in turn was given a taste of the soup and seemed to find it to their liking, each providing one or two little additions which they were convinced would enhance the work of the magic stone. And, sure enough, by the time the kettle was taken off the fire the tramp had it plumb full of the heartiest, zestiest, most tasty soup ever known in the Kickapoo Valley!

Reprinted from Kickapoo Pearls *with the permission of the Kickapoo Valley Association.*

One possible source for the name Milwaukee is the Sioux Indian word "Miniwaki," meaning "firewater." Many people speculate that this name was appropriately suggested by the Great Spirit, who told the Sioux that this city was destined to be the beer capital of the world.

Miniwaki
"A hearty beer cheese soup"

1½ **cups butter**
½ **cup minced celery**
½ **cup grated carrots**
½ **cup finely chopped onions**
½ **cup flour**
4½ **cups chicken broth**
½ **teaspoon dry mustard**
2 **tablespoons Parmesan cheese**
6 **ounces grated Cheddar cheese**
1 **12-ounce can beer**
Salt and pepper to taste

Melt butter in a large saucepan. Sauté vegetables until limp—do not brown. Stir flour into sautéed vegetables all at once and continue stirring, over low heat, until flour expands. Gradually add chicken broth, stirring constantly until thickened. Simmer 5 minutes. Blend in cheeses and beer, stirring constantly, until cheese melts. Add seasonings and simmer 10 minutes.

Serves 6 to 8

Recipes from Wisconsin with Love...

The Kettle Morraine of eastern Wisconsin is a glaciated area of large rounded hills accented by deep hollows. Rising from the top of one of the highest hills is the castle-like Holy Hill Church and monastery. This marks the spot where the paralyzed ex-monk and murderer, Francois Soubris, is said to have spent the night in prayer after climbing the hill on his hands and knees. When the sun rose over the hill, the man was miraculously cured. He lived in a nearby cave until his death, and people still report seeing the hermit's ghost climbing the hill.

Cheezy Zucchini Soup
"Uses a kettle of zucchini"

6 cups water
3 cups chopped yellow onion
3½ pounds zucchini
¼ cup butter
2¼ teaspoons crushed oregano
1½ teaspoons garlic powder
6 ounces grated sharp Cheddar cheese
3 ounces cream cheese
3 tablespoons tamari sauce
¼ teaspoon pepper

Bring water and onion to a boil in a 5-quart kettle. Slice a third of the zucchini and set aside; chop the remainder of the zucchini and add to the boiling water. Cover and cook over medium heat ¾ to 1 hour. (The zucchini should be broken down into the broth.) Add the sliced zucchini, oregano and garlic and bring to a boil again. Reduce heat and simmer 5 to 10 minutes or until zucchini is just tender. Remove 1½ cups of the broth mixture and pour into a blender with cheeses. Blend until smooth; pour back into the broth and stir to blend. Remove from heat and stir in tamari, salt and pepper just before serving.

Serves 4 to 6

Like wild rice, the loon symbolizes wild and beautiful northern Wisconsin. Mercer, in this lake-filled region, claims to be the "loon capital of the world." The aerodynamic loon can fly up to sixty miles per hour and dive as deep as 200 feet, but can barely walk. The female loon lays only two eggs and carries the babies on her back. The haunting call of the loon enchants residents and visitors alike, as does well-prepared wild rice.

Wild Rice-Mushroom Soup

"Company loves it"

3 tablespoons butter or margarine
1 medium onion, finely chopped
3 tablespoons flour
3 cups chicken broth
1 cup sliced, fresh mushrooms*
2 cups cooked wild rice
1 cup half-and-half
¼ to ½ teaspoon salt
Dash of pepper

Melt butter in a large saucepan. Sauté onion. Stir in flour and continue stirring, over low heat, until flour expands. Gradually add chicken broth, stirring constantly until thickened. Add remaining ingredients and heat slowly, stirring often.

*A 3 or 4-ounce can of mushrooms may be substituted for fresh.

Serves 4

The following recipe lets you use up all the stems and small pieces of broccoli. If you have a garden, you can also use those small side shoots. The delicious fresh taste of broccoli complements many meals, or is great by itself.

Blender Broccoli Soup

"Use those odds and ends"

2 cups chopped, fresh
    broccoli
2 cups milk
2 tablespoons butter
    Salt
    Pepper

Blanch broccoli. Drain and place in electric blender with butter and 1 cup of the milk. Whip until nearly smooth. Keep adding milk until desired consistency is reached. Heat to serving temperature; season with desired amount of salt and pepper.

Serves 3 to 4

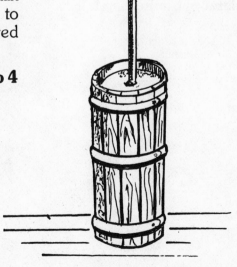

Recipes from Wisconsin with Love...

Many of Paul Bunyan's men were mighty Norwegians. There was Chris Crosshaul, Axel Axelson, Happy Olson, Hels Helsen, Shot Gunderson and Big Ole. Big Ole was the blacksmith who forged the shoes for Babe, the Blue Ox. These shoes were so enormous that they used up all the ore from two iron mines and so heavy that when Ole lifted them he sank knee-deep in solid rock.

Norwegian Fruit Soup
"Frugt Suppe"

½ cup pearl tapioca
¾ cup sugar
3 cups water
1 cup quartered prunes
½ cup currants
1 cup diced apples
1 stick cinnamon
1 cup raisins
¼ teaspoon salt
2 cups grape juice
½ lemon, thinly sliced

Combine all ingredients except grape juice and lemon slices and cook in a heavy saucepan until apples are tender. Add grape juice and lemon slices. Serve hot or cold with ham.

Serves 15

Wisconsin's pride and concern for preservation of its history and natural resources is evident in the number of its state parks. Interstate Park at St. Croix Falls was the first of these and Devil's Lake State Park in the Baraboo Hills attracts the most people every year.

Devil's Lake Salad

1	bunch Romaine lettuce
½	cup olive oil
½	cup vinegar
⅓	cup sugar
¼	teaspoon dry mustard
¼	teaspoon salt
⅛	teaspoon pepper
¼	teaspoon powdered garlic
1	tablespoon worchestershire sauce
⅓	cup grated Parmesan cheese

Garnish:
¼	cup sunflower seeds
⅓	mandarin orange slices
1	medium onion, thinly sliced

Tear lettuce into a salad bowl. Combine oil, vinegar, sugar, mustard, salt, pepper, worchestershire sauce and cheese in a pint jar; shake well. Pour dressing over lettuce just before serving and toss. Garnish with the sunflower seeds, mandarin oranges and onion slices.

Serves 2 to 4

Spinach Salad with Honey Mustard Dressing

"Excellent"

2 bunches spinach
4 green onions
1 large orange
4 slices bacon
6 tablespoons vegetable oil
2 tablespoons cider vinegar
2 tablespoons honey
2 tablespoons Dijon mustard
2 tablespoons toasted sesame seed
1 clove garlic, minced
½ teaspoon fresh ground pepper

Tear spinach into a salad bowl. Chop just the green tops of the onions and toss into spinach. Peel, halve and slice orange; add to spinach. Fry bacon until crisp; drain, crumble and set aside. Shake oil and vinegar together in a jar. Add the remaining ingredients and shake well. Pour over salad, toss and sprinkle crumbled bacon on top.

Serves 4

Lo-Cal Blue Cheese Dressing

½ **cup cold water**
⅓ **cup instant non-fat dry**
    milk granules
1½ **cups small curd**
    cottage cheese
⅓ **cup crumbled**
    blue cheese
3 **tablespoons lemon juice**
¾ **teaspoons onion salt**
¼ **teaspoon garlic salt**

Combine all ingredients in an electric blender; whip until nearly smooth. Cover and chill before serving.

Makes about 2 cups

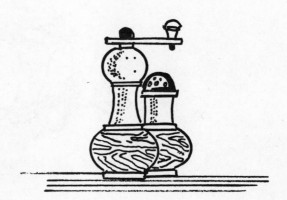

Sonja's Dressing

2 **tablespoons rice vinegar**
¼ **cup olive oil**
3 **cloves garlic, minced**
1 **teaspoon Dijon mustard**
½ **teaspoon salt**
½ **teaspoon pepper**
⅛ **teaspoon sugar**

Combine all ingredients in a pint jar; cover and shake well. Store in the refrigerator.

Makes ⅓ cup

Mary's French Dressing

1 cup catsup
1 small onion, minced*
½ cup vegetable oil
½ cup vinegar
¾ cup sugar

Combine all ingredients in a pint jar. Cover and shake well; refrigerate.

*1 teaspoon dried, minced onion can be substituted.

Wendy's French Dressing

¾ cup sugar
½ cup vinegar
½ cup vegetable oil
½ cup catsup
2 teaspoons paprika
1 clove garlic, minced
1 small onion, finely
   chopped
1 teaspoon salt

Combine all ingredients in a bowl; with an electric mixer, beat several minutes, until well combined. Store in the refrigerator several hours before serving to let the flavors blend.

Makes 1½ cups

Sharp contrasts and great variety grace the state of Wisconsin. The rustic panorama conjured up by the license plate slogan, "America's Dairyland," and idyllic countryside featuring miles of tranquil, rolling hills dotted with black and white spotted cows, certainly is abundant in Wisconsin. But this is just one aspect. It is also a state of industry, centered mostly along the shores of Lake Michigan. It offers diversity of environment and lifestyle ranging from the rural to the multitudes of small, unincorporated villages to the smaller cities and to the one large city, Milwaukee. All of Wisconsin extends its gracious welcome: the bustling metropolis, the academic communities, the peace of natural wilderness, and the many beautiful, multifaceted and accessible recreational areas. They all beckon: "Discover Wisconsin."

Make Ahead Summer Salad

1 head cauliflower
1 bunch broccoli
1 bunch green onions
1 package frozen peas, thawed and drained
1/4 to 1/2 teaspoon salt
1/2 teaspoon garlic salt
1/8 teaspoon pepper
2 cups mayonnaise
1 cup sour cream

Break cauliflower and broccoli into bite-sized pieces; chop onions. Pour peas over cauliflower, broccoli and onions. Combine remaining ingredients and spread over vegetables; toss. Refrigerate in air-tight container overnight.

Serves 8 to 10

Recipes from Wisconsin with Love...

Where the Wisconsin and Mississippi Rivers meet sits Prairie du Chien, the state's second oldest city. It was the site of North America's largest gathering of Indians in 1829. At that same time it was a leading fur trading post and rendezvous site, largely due to the efforts of Hercules Louis Dousman, agent of the Astor Fur Company. Here he built his extravagant Victorian mansion, Villa Louis, which can be seen today still filled with many of its original rare and valuable furnishings.

Prairie Salad
"Fresh and crunchy"

1   bunch broccoli
1   head cauliflower
½   cup raisins
½   pound bacon, fried, drained and crumbled*
¼   cup minced onions
½   cup sunflower seeds
½   cup mayonnaise
2   tablespoons vinegar
2   tablespoons sugar
2   teaspoons milk

Break broccoli and cauliflower into bite-sized pieces. Add raisins, bacon, onions and sunflower seeds. Combine mayonnaise, vinegar, sugar and milk; spread over vegetables and toss. Refrigerate at least two hours before serving.

*Chopped turkey, chicken or other meat may be substituted.

Serves 8 to 10

Broccoli Salad
"Great for summer-time eating"

2 pounds fresh broccoli
¼ cup chopped green onions
¾ cup halved pimento-stuffed olives
1 cup mayonnaise
1 teaspoon dill weed
¼ to ½ teaspoon salt
⅛ teaspoon pepper
2 hard boiled eggs, sliced

Steam broccoli 5 minutes until bright green but still crisp; cool and cut into ½-inch pieces. Add onions and olives. Combine mayonnaise and seasonings; spread over vegetables and toss well. Refrigerate 24 hours. Toss with slices of egg just before serving.

Serves 6 to 8

Much of Wisconsin's unique character comes from the immigrants who settled it. One common belief is that "Wisconsin is progressive because of cheese, peas and Germans."

Mixed Pea Salad

"Very progressive"

1 medium cucumber
2 10-ounce packages frozen baby peas, thawed and drained
3 tablespoons minced fresh mint*
1/2 cup mayonnaise
1 tablespoon lime or lemon juice
1 tablespoon honey
1/2 teaspoon salt
Lettuce leaves
Mint sprigs

Pare, halve lengthwise and seed cucumber; chop and combine with peas and minced mint. Blend together the mayonnaise, lime juice, honey and salt; pour over vegetables and toss well. Serve individually on lettuce leaves and garnish with mint sprigs.

*1/2 teaspoon crushed dried mint leaves may be substituted.

Serves 6 to 8

Recipes from Wisconsin with Love . . .

The ethnic mix of Milwaukee is a broad one, with over 50 nationalities represented there. In honor of this intriguing variety which is so essential to its character, the city celebrates each year before Thanksgiving with the "Holiday Folk Fair." Sponsored by the International Institute of Milwaukee County, it is the largest international folk festival in the nation. This entertaining and interesting event features outstanding cultural exhibits, international cuisine, a world shopping mart, ethnic entertainment and an Old World beer garden.

Oriental Cucumber Salad

1 large cucumber
1 teaspoon salt
1 cup sugar
1 cup white vinegar
1 teaspoon monosodium glutamate (MSG)

Slice cucumber paper thin; rub salt in and set aside ½ hour. Strain through a cheesecloth and squeeze out juice. Combine sugar, vinegar and MSG; pour over cucumbers. Set aside 15 minutes; strain through a cheesecloth and squeeze to remove juice. Serve with more dressing, if desired.

Serves 3 to 6

The existence of the lumberjacks was difficult and dangerous, and their ballads were often reflections of the harsh realities of their lives and their deaths, filled with the phrases of their own special language. The Wisconsin version of this sad and sentimental ballad is well-founded in fact.

"The Log Jam on Gerry's Rocks"

Come all you true born shanty-boys wherever you may be
Come sit here on the deacon's seat, and listen unto me.
It's about a gay young shanty-boy, so gentle, strong, and brave,
Was at the jam on Gerry's rocks, he met a watery grave.

Was on a Sunday morning, as you shall plainly hear,
The logs were piled high, we could not get them clear.
"Turn out brave boys!" Monroe did cry, his voice devoid of fear.
"We'll break the jam on Gerry's rocks and for Eagleston we'll steer."

They had not pushed off many logs, before Monroe did say:
"I'd have you all be on your guard, this jam will soon give way."
He had no more than spoke these words before the jam did go,
And swept away those six brave youths, and foreman young Monroe.

When the rest of all the shanty-boys the sad news came to hear,
They gathered up the river boys and downward they did steer.
And there they found to their surprise and sorrow, grief, and woe,
All cut and mangled on the shore, the form of young Monroe.

They picked him from the water, pushed back his raven black hair
There was one fair form among them all whose cries did rend the air
There was one fair form among them all, a girl from Oshkosh town,
Whose mournful cries did rend the air, for her lover who was drowned.

Recipes from Wisconsin with Love...

The State Historical Society of Wisconsin was founded in 1846 and is dedicated to "the collection, advancement, and dissemination of knowledge of the history of Wisconsin." It began operating living historical sites in 1952 and now has seven: Stonefield near Cassville; Pendarvis in Mineral Point; Old World Wisconsin, an outdoor ethnic museum near Eagle; Madeline Island Historical Museum in LaPointe; Villa Louis in Prairie du Chien; the Old Wade House Historical Site at Greenbush; and the Circus World Museum in Baraboo. In addition to the main facility in Madison, it maintains Area Research Centers on 13 campuses around the state. Through their efforts the fruits of history are gathered for us to relish.

Historic Fruit Salad
"Out of site"

1 6-ounce package strawberry gelatin
1 cup boiling water
3 medium bananas, mashed
2 10-ounce packages frozen strawberries, thawed and drained
1 20-ounce can crushed pineapple, drained
1 pint sour cream

Combine gelatin and water, stirring until gelatin is completely dissolved. Cool. Add bananas, strawberries and pineapple, stirring to distribute evenly. Pour half the gelatin mixture into a 9 x 13-inch baking pan; refrigerate until partially set. (Remaining gelatin should be kept at room temperature.) Spread sour cream evenly over jelled mixture and pour remaining gelatin on top. Cover and refrigerate until set.

12 Servings

Recipes from Wisconsin with Love...

Mary Michalski started her climb to international stage and screen fame at Pulaski Hall in Cudahy. Creating ripples far and wide under the stage name of Gilda Gray, she perfected the "shimmy" in the 1920's.

Apricot Shimmy

1 **16-ounce can crushed pineapple**
¾ **cup sugar**
1 **3-ounce package apricot or peach gelatin**
8 **ounces cream cheese**
5 **tablespoons milk**
1 **cup whipping cream**
½ **teaspoon vanilla**

Combine undrained pineapple and ½ cup sugar in a heavy saucepan; bring to a boil. Remove from heat and stir in gelatin. Cool and refrigerate just until mixture is thick and beginning to set. Blend cream cheese and milk; beat until smooth. Beat whipping cream until thick, add remaining ¼ cup sugar and vanilla, and continue beating until stiff. Combine the thickened gelatin, cream cheese mixture and whipped cream, folding until well blended. Pour into a lightly oiled 2-quart mold and refrigerate until set. Invert onto a bed of lettuce or parsley to serve.

Serves 6

The robin announces spring to the people of Wisconsin. What better choice for the state bird? With the arrival of spring and the robin comes the desire for salads and refreshing foods. Enjoy the following salad.

Grapefruit-Cherry Salad

"A harbinger of spring"

1 **16-ounce can grapefruit sections, drained**
1 **15-ounce can dark sweet cherries, drained**
1 **3-ounce package lime gelatin**
1 **cup boiling water**
1 **cup ginger ale**

Arrange grapefruit sections and cherries in alternate layers in a lightly oiled ring mold. Dissolve gelatin in boiling water; cool. Stir in ginger ale. Pour gelatin over layered fruit and chill until firm. Invert onto a bed of lettuce leaves.

4 to 6 Servings

Cranberry Nut Crunch Salad
"Add a little color to your meal"

3 **envelopes unflavored gelatin**
¾ **cup cold water**
3 **16-ounce cans jelled cranberry sauce**
2½ **cups chopped walnuts**
6 **bananas, diced**

Combine gelatin and water in top of double boiler; stir over boiler water to dissolve. Beat cranberry sauce. Blend in nuts and bananas. Fold in softened gelatin. Pour mixture into a lightly oiled 2-quart ring mold and refrigerate until set. Unmold onto a bed of lettuce leaves.

Serves 12

Dutchmans Breeches

Caddie Woodlawn is known and loved by children throughout the world. Her adventures in the books *Caddie Woodlawn* and its sequel, *Magical Melons,* are based on the life of Caroline Augusta Woodhouse. The author, Carol Ryrie Brink, faithfully recreates her grandmother's memorable childhood in pioneer Menomonie. In 1935, *Caddie Woodlawn* received the Newberry Award as "the most distinguished children's book of the year."

Magical Melons with Poppyseed Dressing

1 large honeydew or cantelope
6 cups bite-sized fresh fruit

Poppyseed Dressing:
  1 cup whipping cream
  ⅓ cup mayonnaise*
  ¼ cup honey
  2 tablespoons poppyseeds
  1 teaspoon lemon juice

Quarter and seed melon; arrange a cup or more of fruit in each. Combine whipping cream and mayonnaise; blend well. Add honey, poppyseeds and lemon juice, stirring to blend. Spoon over fruit and serve. Store dressing, covered, in the refrigerator.

*Dressing can be used as a dip by substituting 3 ounces cream cheese for the mayonnaise.

Serves 4

Over 100 circuses originated in Wisconsin. For many years Delevan provided the winter home for 26 of them. The now standard 3-ring circus was first devised in Delevan by W. C. Coup.

3-Ring Salad
"A hard act to follow"

2   or 3 bananas, sliced
1   20-ounce can pineapple
    chunks
2   11-ounce cans mandarin
    orange segments
1   3¼-ounce package
    vanilla pudding and
    pie filling

Drain pineapple chunks, reserving liquid. Combine banana slices, orange sections and pineapple. Blend together the pudding mix and reserved pineapple juice; cook over medium heat, stirring constantly, just until mixture starts to boil. Cool and pour over fruits. Chill, covered, in a salad bowl or in individual parfait glasses.

4 Servings

Vegetables and Side Dishes

Recipes from Wisconsin with Love...

Nelson Dewey first arrived in Cassville in 1836. After serving as the first Governor of Wisconsin, he returned to Cassville, where he put down his roots in a 2000-acre plantation which he called Stonefield. Today, Stonefield is the State Farm Museum, highlighting various aspects of farming on the frontier. A confirmed agrarian and vegetable-lover, Nelson Dewey would undoubtedly have found Veggie Pizza an agreeable recipe.

Veggie Pizza

"A vote-winner"

2 8-ounce tubes
  commercial
  crescent rolls
1 cup mayonnaise
⅓ cup sour cream
16 ounces cream cheese
¼ teaspoon dill
  Chopped broccoli
  Sliced radishes
  Chopped green onions
  Thinly sliced green
  pepper
  Sliced zucchini
  Chopped cauliflower
  Sliced mushrooms
8 ounces grated Cheddar
  cheese

Unroll dough onto a greased cookie sheet, press the perforations together and pinch edges up to make a ridge. Bake in a 375° oven 12 to 15 minutes or until lightly browned. Cool. Combine mayonnaise, sour cream, cream cheese and dill; mix until well blended. Spread on cooled crust. Top with any combination of vegetables desired, using no more than a total of 6 cups. Sprinkle Cheddar cheese on top. Bake 12 to 15 minutes, just until cheese melts and vegetables are hot.

Serves 4 to 6

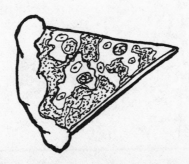

State Street in Madison offers the pedestrian eight blocks of delightful hodgepodge. The Mall connecting the University to the Capitol has an atmosphere that is relaxed though bustling with activity. Street vendors, musicians and a medley of shops and restaurants all mingle together in a wonderful community feeling.

Garden Ratatouille
"Vegetable hodgepodge"

3 or 4 slices bacon, chopped
2 cloves garlic, minced
1 medium onion, chopped
½ pound broccoli, sliced into small spears*
1 green pepper, seeded and sliced
1 or 2 small zucchini, sliced
Dash of pepper
¼ teaspoon salt
2 small tomatoes, cut in wedges
½ cup grated Parmesan cheese

Fry bacon over low heat until crisp; reserving fat, drain bacon on paper toweling. In bacon fat, sauté garlic and onion. Add broccoli and green pepper and cook, covered, 2 minutes. Add zucchini, salt and pepper, cover and cook another 5 minutes. Add tomato wedges and cook, covered, just until vegetables are tender and hot. Do not overcook. Sprinkle with cheese and bacon. Broil for 1 or 2 minutes, until cheese is lightly toasted.

*Cauliflower flowerets may be substituted.

Serves 4 to 6

Recipes from Wisconsin with Love...

The strong commitment to higher education is evident in the large number of private and public colleges and universities in the state. The University of Wisconsin, established in 1849 in space rented at the Madison Female Academy, has grown into a network of campuses. These are very closely involved in the agriculture, forestry and politics of their respective areas. The University has earned much acclaim for its experimental work in cultivating these fields.

Carrot Ring

"Impressive"

2 cups cooked, mashed carrots
½ teaspoon grated onion
3 eggs, beaten
1 cup milk
2 tablespoons melted butter or margarine
1 teaspoon salt
¼ teaspoon pepper
  Cooked, buttered peas

Combine all ingredients except peas and stir well. Pour into a heavily greased 1-quart ring mold. Place mold in a baking pan filled with water and bake in a 350° oven 45 to 50 minutes. Cool at room temperature 10 minutes, loosen edges and carefully unmold onto a platter. Fill center with cooked peas.

Serves 6 to 8

Broccoli Rice Bake

1½ cups cooked rice
2 tablespoons margarine
½ cup chopped celery
½ cup chopped onion
4 cups cooked, drained chopped broccoli
1 10¾-ounce can cream of chicken soup
¼ cup water
1 8-ounce jar Cheese Whiz™
1 cup cooked, diced ham or turkey

Melt butter; sauté celery and onion. Combine all the ingredients and mix well. Bake in 350° oven 25 to 30 minutes or until bubbly.

Serves 6

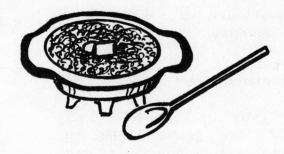

Anti-slavery sentiment ran high in Wisconsin in the mid-1800's. Prominent people, religious groups, small organizations and ordinary people all worked together to form a network called "The Underground Railroad." Escaped slaves were spirited from one house to another on their way to Canada, pursued by indignant slave owners or their agents.

Baked Parsnips Au Gratin
"Give this vegetable a break"

2 pounds parsnips
¼ cup butter
2 tablespoons flour
1½ cups milk
½ teaspoon salt
⅛ teaspoon pepper
½ cup bread crumbs
⅓ cup grated sharp
　 Cheddar cheese

Pare and cube parsnips; simmer in lightly salted water 10 to 15 minutes just until tender. Melt 2 tablespoons of the butter in a saucepan. Stir flour into butter and continue stirring for one minute. Gradually add milk, stirring constantly until thickened. Add seasonings and simmer one minute. Mix together parsnips and sauce and pour into a greased 1½-quart casserole. Brown bread crumbs in the remaining 2 tablespoons butter. Remove from heat and toss with grated cheese; sprinkle over parsnips. Bake 25 to 30 minutes in a 350° oven.

Serves 6 to 8

Gratin of Sliced Tomato

1 **pound ripe tomatoes, skinned and sliced**
4 **teaspoons dry sherry**
2 **teaspoons minced fresh basil**
½ **cup whipping cream**
⅛ **teaspoon salt**
   Dash of pepper
¾ **cup grated Cheddar cheese**
   Parsley, minced

Divide tomato slices into 4 buttered ramekins; sprinkle with sherry and basil. Bake 30 minutes in a 300° oven. Combine cream, salt and pepper; add two tablespoons of the seasoned cream to each ramekin and sprinkle evenly with the cheese. Bake 15 minutes, garnish with parsley and serve.

Serves 4

Recipes from Wisconsin with Love...

In 1885 a new and unique type of cheese was developed by Joseph Steinwand. Named for the township, Colby is a mild, soft, moist cheese, which has become a universal favorite. Wisconsin, currently first in U.S. production of almost every cheese, is also the birthplace of Brick cheese.

Tomato Cheese Pie

3 tablespoons olive oil
1 clove garlic, minced
3 pounds ripe tomatoes, skinned, seeded and coarsely chopped
¾ teaspoon salt
2 tablespoons chopped fresh parsley
½ teaspoon crushed basil
Pepper, freshly ground
3 or 4 large yellow onions, thickly sliced
2 tablespoons butter
⅓ cup grated Parmesan cheese
1 baked pastry shell for an 11-inch quiche pan
½ pound grated Mozzarella cheese
12 black olives, sliced

Heat oil and sauté garlic several minutes. Stir in tomatoes, ½ teaspoon of the salt, parsley, basil and several gratings of pepper. Simmer, stirring occasionally, until sauce is quite thick. Sauté onion slices in butter until golden; sprinkle with remaining salt. Sprinkle the Parmesan cheese over bottom of pastry shell. Arrange the onions over the cheese in even layers. Cover onions with the tomato sauce. Sprinkle Mozzarella evenly over the tomato sauce and arrange the olive slices on top. Bake in a preheated 375° oven 35 minutes.

Makes 1 pie

Recipes from Wisconsin with Love...

There is a belief at Cave Point in Door County that one of the caves extends under the peninsula to the Green Bay side, ten miles away. As proof, when a steamer loaded with corn was wrecked and washed ashore near this cave, corn was later found floating almost directly opposite on the Green Bay side.

Cave Point Scalloped Corn
"Kids love it"

2 eggs
1 cup milk
1 16-ounce can cream
   style corn
1/2 cup saltine cracker
   crumbs
1/2 teaspoon baking powder
1/8 teaspoon salt*

Combine eggs and milk in a 1-quart casserole; beat well. Add corn, cracker crumbs, baking powder and salt, stirring to blend well. Bake in 375° oven 1 hour or until top is crusty and slightly browned.

*optional

Serves 4 to 6

Farmers have many theories about the proper times to plant crops. Most of these are related to the cycles of the moon or the weather. Wisconsin farmers say that the ideal time to plant corn is when the young oak leaves are the size of a squirrel's ear.

Corn Pudding
"They love this one too!"

2 eggs
½ cup milk
  Dash of sugar
  Dash of salt
2 tablespoons flour
2 or 3 tablespoons melted
  butter
1 16-ounce can cream
  style corn

Beat eggs well; stir in milk, sugar, salt and flour and beat until smooth. Blend in butter and corn. Pour into a greased 1-quart casserole. Bake in 350° oven for 1 hour or until set.

Serves 4 to 6

Recipes from Wisconsin with Love...

Prehistoric Indian tribes in Wisconsin have been traced as far back as 8000 years to those of the Copper Culture, whose ceremonial grounds have been found near Oconto. There are vestiges of an intriguing and isolated alien tribe of cannibal dwellers called the Aztalan who took up residence for a brief time near Lake Mills. Believed to be related to the Aztecs of Mexico, this tribe built their archaeologically amazing pyramid-shaped mounds inside a walled-in fortress. But by far the most prevalent ancient remnants found in Wisconsin today are the mounds of the Effigy Mound People, with more found here than in any other state. Most of the prehistoric tribes did build mounds and these low formations were often built in the shapes of animals, birds and reptiles. Near Baraboo is the famous "Man Mound," shaped like a 150-foot man in repose. Fort Atkinson has the only known intaglio effigy in the world, carved into the shape of a panther. These and many other mound sites around Wisconsin have been preserved as parks, and can be seen by the public.

Baked Pumpkin

"A mound of flavor"

1 18-ounce can pumpkin
1 egg
3 tablespoons melted butter
3 tablespoons evaporated milk
¼ teaspoon salt
¼ teaspoon nutmeg
¼ teaspoon allspice
2 or 3 tablespoons sugar

Combine all ingredients and beat well. Pour into a buttered 1½-quart casserole. Bake in a 350° oven 30 to 35 minutes or until top is lightly browned and mixture is set.

Serves 4

Recipes from Wisconsin with Love...

"Escape to Wisconsin" the slogan beckons. Tourism is one of the major industries in Wisconsin, where the many lakes and rivers, the hilly terrain and the grand forests are hospitable to the wide variety of sports and recreation which accompany each season.

Spinach Pie

2 cups grated sharp Cheddar cheese
2 tablespoons flour
4 eggs
1 cup milk
½ teaspoon salt
1 10-ounce package frozen, chopped spinach, thawed
Dash of pepper
1 unbaked pastry shell for a 9-inch pie

Toss cheese with flour. Beat together eggs, milk and seasonings. Stir in cheese. Drain thawed spinach on paper toweling; add to egg mixture with cheese. Mix well. Pour into pastry shell and bake in 350° oven 40 minutes or until knife inserted in center comes out clean. Note: if desired, meats like bacon or ham can be added with the spinach to make a main dish.

6 Servings

Spinach Casserole

"Popeye would approve"

3 eggs
1 13-ounce can
 evaporated milk
¼ cup melted butter or
 margarine
3 cups cooked rice
4 ounces grated Cheddar
 cheese
½ teaspoon salt
¼ teaspoon pepper
1 10-ounce package
 frozen chopped spinach,
 thawed and drained

Beat eggs; add milk, butter, rice, cheese and seasonings. Stir well. Add drained spinach and stir again. Pour into a greased slow cooker and cook on high setting 1 hour. Turn to low and cook 5 hours. Alternatively, pour into a greased 2-quart casserole and bake in a 350° oven 35 minutes or until hot and bubbly.

Serves 6 to 8

Recipes from Wisconsin with Love...

When August rolls around, zucchini abounds, and people look to un-suspecting friends and neighbors to take some off their hands. One woman in Antigo says she grows one zucchini plant "just for protec-tion" against this sort of thing. Here is a simple, satisfying recipe that will help you use your plentiful produce in a nutritious way.

Zucchini Again

"And again... and again... and again..."

1 tablespoon vegetable oil
3 cups pared, cubed zucchini
1 large onion, sliced
1 large green pepper, sliced
4 medium, stewed tomatoes*
1 4-ounce can mushrooms
½ teaspoon salt
¼ teaspoon pepper
½ to 1 teaspoon crushed oregano leaves
¼ to ½ teaspoon crushed basil leaves
½ to 1 teaspoon garlic powder
½ to 1 cup grated Mozzarella cheese

Heat oil in a large skillet. Stir in zucchini, brown lightly and cook 5 to 8 minutes. Add onion, green pepper, tomatoes, mushrooms and seasonings; stir well to blend. Cover and simmer 15 minutes or until vegetables are tender. Sprinkle cheese over vegetables, reduce heat and cover until cheese is melted. Serve with garlic bread or plain French bread.

*½ cup tomato sauce can be substituted for stewed tomatoes.

Serves 4

Maple syrup can often replace brown sugar in cooking, enhancing even the most common of recipes with its distinctive flavor and nutritional merits. In the early days, maple syrup and maple sugar were often the only sweeteners available to the pioneers.

Baked Squash with Maple Syrup

2 medium acorn squash
¼ cup butter
¼ cup pure maple syrup
   Salt
   Pepper
½ teaspoon cinnamon*
¼ teaspoon nutmeg*
¼ teaspoon cloves*

Halve and seed squash; pierce several times with a fork. Arrange in a shallow baking dish, hollowed side up. Dot each hollow with 1 tablespoon butter topped by 1 tablespoon syrup. Season as desired. Pour 1 inch of boiling water into pan and bake in 375° oven 1 hour or until squash is tender, adding more boiling water as necessary.

*optional

Serves 4

Recipes from Wisconsin with Love...

Vegetables are a main source of income for many of Wisconsin's farmers. Wisconsin ranks high in the production of carrots, sweet corn, red beets, cabbage and snap beans for canning. The following casserole is a tasty variation of the more common bean and mushroom soup theme.

Green Bean Casserole

"A variation on a theme"

2 16-ounce cans green beans
1 10 ¾ ounce can Cheddar cheese soup
1 3-ounce can mushrooms drained and sliced
1 cup grated Cheddar cheese

Combine undrained beans and soup; add mushrooms and blend well. Pour into a greased 1 or 1½-quart casserole and sprinkle with cheese. Bake uncovered in a 350° oven 20 minutes.

Serves 6 to 8

Frank Lloyd Wright, world-renowned architect, was born in Richland Center. This colorful and controversial artist endowed his native state with many fine examples of his work, five of which are listed in the National Register of Historic Places. The Warehouse, a red brick structure completed in his hometown in 1920, opened to the public in 1982 and now houses the Frank Lloyd Wright Museum. Nearby in Spring Green stands Taliesen, Wright's architectural school and home. Both the Warehouse and Taliesen are examples of his organic or natural period of architecture.

Noodles and Cabbage with Sour Cream and Poppy Seed

3 cups uncooked egg noodles
¼ cup butter or margarine
2 to 3 cups shredded cabbage
2 to 3 chopped green onions, with tops*
1 teaspoon poppy seeds
Dash of pepper
¼ teaspoon salt
½ cup sour cream

Cook noodles just until tender, drain and keep warm. Steam cabbage just until hot. (Cabbage should be crisp but tender.) Melt butter in large skillet and sauté onions. Stir in noodles, poppy seeds and seasonings. Stir in sour cream. Add cabbage, stirring to coat evenly with sauce. Chicken or ham can be added to make this into a main dish.

*A minced garlic clove can be substituted for the onions.

Serves 8

FRANK LLOYD WRIGHT DESIGNED

THE WAREHOUSE

Recipes from Wisconsin with Love...

Winneconne, "the place of skulls," was named after an Indian battle. A cartographer's oversight left the town off the Wisconsin road map in 1967. This graphic displacement made the citizens so sour that they seceded from the state for two days, until they were restored to their rightful position. Their protest was registered in the following poem: "Wisconsin must have had a mental lapse, To take Winneconne off the highway maps."

Sour Cream Potatoes

"Puts your kitchen on the map"

6 medium potatoes
1 pint sour cream
1½ cups grated Cheddar cheese
1 green onion, chopped
3 tablespoons milk
1 teaspoon salt
⅛ teaspoon pepper
2 tablespoons melted butter
⅓ cup bread crumbs

Cook potatoes in lightly salted water; drain and chill. Peel potatoes and coarsely grate. Add sour cream, cheese, onion, milk, and seasonings. Spread mixture in a greased 9 x 13-inch baking pan. Mix together butter and bread crumbs and sprinkle on top. Bake in 300° oven 50 minutes.

8 Servings

Recipes from Wisconsin with Love...

The Green Bay Packer Hall of Fame chronicles the history of this illustrious team, paying tribute to its members, past and present. The Packers led the National Football League in total wins, having gained the title 11 times. They're the only team to have won three consecutive titles, a feat they've accomplished twice! They have also won two Super Bowls. Is it any wonder the whole nation quakes at the cry, "The Pack is Back!"?

Potato Pancakes
"Sure to fill a hungry football fan!"

3 eggs
1 teaspoon salt
1 tablespoon sugar
3 cups milk
2 tablespoons melted shortening
2½ cups flour
3 cups grated uncooked potatoes

Combine eggs, salt, sugar, milk and shortening; beat well. Gradually add flour, beating well. Stir in potatoes. Pour 1 heaping tablespoon of batter per serving onto medium hot griddle greased with a few drops of oil. Fry 3 minutes on each side.

Makes 2 dozen

Recipes from Wisconsin with Love...

The Germans make up the largest ethnic group in Wisconsin. This recipe came from one of Wisconsin's very traditional families.

Baked German Potato Salad

1 cup diced bacon
1 cup sliced celery
1 cup chopped onion
3 teaspoons salt
3 tablespoons flour
⅔ cup sugar
⅔ cup vinegar
½ teaspoon pepper
1⅓ cups water
8 cups cooked, sliced potatoes

Fry bacon; drain on paper toweling. Pour all but ¼ cup bacon grease from skillet. Add celery, onion, salt and flour; simmer, stirring constantly. Add sugar, vinegar, pepper and water and bring to a boil. Toss bacon and potatoes together in a 3-quart baking dish; pour hot mixture over potatoes. Cover and bake in 350° oven for 30 minutes.

Serves 12

Recipes from Wisconsin with Love...

As with any new territory, Wisconsin required a little parenting on its way to becoming a state. Charles deLanglade earned the honor as "Father of Wisconsin" in 1745 when he came to the Green Bay area, creating the oldest settlement in Wisconsin. DeLanglade's influence helped shape Wisconsin's early history and paved the road for its territorial status in 1836. On May 29, 1848, Wisconsin graduated as the 30th state, indebted to deLanglade's early guidance.

Dad's Rice and Cheese Bake

1 cup uncooked rice
⅓ cup diced Provolone
⅓ cup diced Bel Paese or Brick cheese
⅓ cup diced Gruyere or Swiss cheese
⅔ cup freshly grated Parmesan cheese
½ cup chopped ham
¼ teaspoon salt
⅛ teaspoon pepper
Butter

Cook rice in several cups rapidly boiling water for 15 minutes until nearly done. Rinse with cold water and drain. Combine Provolone, Bal Paese, Gruyere, half the Parmesan cheese and ham. Toss drained rice with salt and pepper and spread a third onto the bottom of a buttered 1½-quart casserole. Arrange half the cheese and ham over the rice; repeat layers, ending with rice on top. Dot casserole with butter and the remaining ⅓ cup Parmesan. Set casserole in a pan of water and bake in 350° oven 20 minutes. Uncover and bake an additional 5 minutes or until the Parmesan on top is golden.

Serves 4

Rice with Maple Syrup

1 cup uncooked rice
2 teaspoons margarine or butter
2 cups water
½ teaspoon salt
¼ to ½ cup maple syrup

Sauté rice in butter several minutes until butter is absorbed. Add water and salt, bring to a boil, reduce heat, cover and cook until water is absorbed and rice is done. Pour syrup evenly over rice; let steep several minutes. Toss lightly and serve.

Serves 3 to 4

Menomonee County became the 72nd and newest county of Wisconsin as recently as 1961. It was only then that the U.S. Government gave up its claims to the lands of the Menomonee Indian Reservation. The properties of the Menomonees were made into a corporation, with the individuals of the tribe holding shares. The name Menomonee means "People of the Wild Rice."

Wild Rice Casserole

1 cup uncooked wild rice
½ cup chopped celery
½ cup chopped green pepper
½ cup butter or margarine
3 13½-ounce cans beef broth

Rinse rice under cold water until clean; turn into a buttered 1½-quart casserole. Sauté celery and green pepper in butter; mix with rice. Pour broth over rice, using just enough to cover. Bake in 350° oven, covered, 1½ hours, adding reserved broth as necessary, to keep rice from drying out.

Serves 4 to 6

The Chippewa Indians call wild rice the "Good Berry." Actually, it is neither a rice nor a berry, but an aquatic grass.

Wild Raspberry.

Good Berry Casserole

1 4-ounce can mushroom
   stems and pieces
½ cup butter or margarine
1 cup chopped celery
½ cup chopped onion
4 cups cooked wild rice
1 13½-ounce can cream of
   mushroom soup
1 teaspoon salt
⅛ to ¼ teaspoon pepper

Sauté mushrooms in butter 10 minutes. Remove mushrooms from butter; sauté celery and onion until onions are golden. Mix together sautéed vegetables with rice, add remaining ingredients and stir well. Cover and bake in 350° oven 35 to 40 minutes.

Serves 6

Recipes from Wisconsin with Love...

Rice Lake is one of the best natural wild rice stands in the world. The ricing is still done by pushing and poling the canoe and tapping the ripened kernels with a long stick into the bottom of the canoe. The rice harvesting still provides an opportunity for the Chippewa people to gather according to time-honored traditions to work, celebrate and rekindle the fires of their ancestors with ancient legends and songs.

Chippewa Wild Rice

1 **cup uncooked wild rice**
2½ **cups water**
1½ **teaspoons salt**
4 **strips bacon**
6 **eggs**
¼ **teaspoon pepper**
2 **tablespoons minced chives**

Rinse rice under cold water to clean. Stir into a large saucepan with water and 1 teaspoon of salt; bring to a boil, reduce heat and simmer until water is absorbed. Meanwhile, cut bacon into julienne strips and slowly cook in a skillet. Reserving drippings in a small bowl, drain bacon on paper toweling. Beat eggs with remaining ½ teaspoon salt and pepper. Pour into skillet and cook over low heat until underside is lightly browned; flip and brown the other side (eggs should be firmly cooked at the end of this step). Cut eggs into julienne strips, lightly toss with bacon, chives and rice. Combine enough melted butter with the reserved bacon drippings to make ⅓ cup. Drizzle over rice mixture and toss again.

Serves 4 to 6

Main Dishes

Recipes from Wisconsin with Love...

The only thing that distinguishes Booyah from chicken soup is that Booyah contains such large chunks. To this day, it is a fund-raising favorite of churches and clubs, who naturally prepare it in gargantuan batches, cooked to perfection through the collaboration of many seasoned chefs, sippers and tasters.

Booyah
"An old German recipe"

1 chicken
2 large onions, cut in wedges
4 large carrots, cut in 1-inch chunks
½ bunch celery, cut in 1-inch chunks
3 large potatoes, cut in 1-inch chunks
1 to 2 teaspoons salt
½ to 1 teaspoon pepper
1 to 2 cups egg noodles

Place whole chicken in a large kettle and pour in a gallon or more water to cover well. Add onion wedges and bring to a boil. Boil chicken 1 hour or until tender and about to fall from the bone. Lift chicken from broth with tongs or large forks and cool. Reduce heat under broth. De-bone chicken, cutting into large chunks where necessary. Return chicken to broth and add carrots, celery and potatoes. Bring broth back to a boil, season to taste with salt and pepper and cook 1 hour or longer. About 20 minutes before serving, add noodles and boil until noodles are tender.

Serves 10

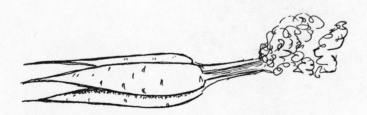

Pineapple Chicken

1 **3-pound chicken, quartered or cut in parts**
1 **20-ounce can unsweetened pineapple chunks**
1 **tablespoon tamari***
3 **tablespoons red wine vinegar**
½ **teaspoon dry mustard**
⅛ **teaspoon cayenne**
1 **green pepper, seeded and coarsely chopped**

Arrange chicken in a baking dish. Combine undrained pineapple, tamari, vinegar, mustard and cayenne; pour over chicken. Bake in 350° oven 45 minutes; add green pepper and bake an additional 15 minutes.

*Regular soy sauce can be substituted for the tamari.

Serves 4 to 6

Recipes from Wisconsin with Love...

An eminent and beloved figure in Wisconsin history was Old Abe, a majestic eagle who was named after his well-known contemporary. Captured at Jim Falls in 1861, he was purchased for a bushel of corn by an old fiddler who instilled in him a love of army songs. It was natural, then, that he should be a candidate for induction in the military, and Company C of the 8th Wisconsin Battery of Eau Claire bought him from the fiddler for $5. Old Abe went into 42 battles during the Civil War, and starred in numerous parades around the country. It is reported that his conduct in battle was magnificent and inspirational. Following the war, he was presented to the State of Wisconsin, which declined a $20,000 offer from P. T. Barnum, and instead raised money for war charities by selling Abe's feathers for as much as $400 each. Abe resided in his own special room in the basement of the Capitol in Madison until a fire broke out in the building. His shrieks brought rescuers who saved him from burning, but Old Abe died later from the effects of smoke inhalation, on March 26, 1881. With a taxidermist's assistance Abe resumed his place of honor in the Capitol until a second fire sent his remains skyward in a blaze of glory. Among his favorite tricks during his long and eventful life was stealing chickens from the regimental cook.

Old Abe's Chicken Parm

2 pounds quartered or cut up chicken
1 10¾-ounce can tomato soup
¼ cup water
¼ cup minced onions
1 clove garlic, minced or mashed
¼ teaspoon oregano
4 ounces grated Mozzarella cheese
2 tablespoons grated Parmesan cheese

Arrange chicken, skin side down, in a 9 x 13-inch baking pan and bake in 400° oven 30 minutes. Turn and bake an additional 30 minutes. Combine soup, water, onions, garlic and oregano, blending well. Pour over chicken and sprinkle with cheeses. Reduce oven temperature to 300° and bake 20 minutes or until cheese is lightly browned. The sauce can be doubled to make enough to serve with pasta or rice.

4 Servings

Shaped like a Greek Cross, the imposing state capitol building crowns a hill surrounded by Lakes Monona and Mendota. Surmounting its tall dome is a stately gilded bronze woman, symbolizing the State Motto, "Forward." From this vantage point, she surveys the city and surrounding countryside for miles around, the beauty of which is so stirring that it moved Longfellow to write his poem, "The Four Lakes of Madison."

Madison Chicken

1 2½-pound chicken, quartered or cut up
½ teaspoon seasoned salt
¼ teaspoon pepper
¾ 8-ounce bottle low calorie Italian salad dressing

Season chicken and arrange in a baking pan. Pour dressing over chicken. Bake in 350° oven, basting often, 1 hour.

Serves 4 to 5

The Four Lakes of Madison

Four limpid lakes, — four Naiades
Or sylvan deities are these,
In flowing robes of azure dressed;
Four lovely handmaids, that uphold
Their shining mirrors, rimmed with gold,
To the fair city in the West.

By day the coursers of the sun
Drink of these waters as they run
Their swift diurnal round on high;
By night the constellations glow
Far down the hollow deeps below,
And glimmer in another sky.

Fair lakes, serene and full of light,
Fair town, arrayed in robes of white,
How visionary ye appear!
All like a floating landscape seems
In cloud-land or the land of dreams,
Bathed in a golden atmosphere!

Henry Wadsworth Longfellow

Scallopini with Balsamella Sauce
"Decadent"

4 **large boneless chicken breasts**
4 **slices prosciutto ham**
4 **slices Swiss cheese**
½ **pound fresh mushrooms**
½ **cup flour**
¼ **cup butter**
1 **cup dry white wine or vermouth**
⅛ **teaspoon white pepper**
¼ **teaspoon salt**
  Lemon slices and parsley

Flatten chicken between sheets of waxed paper with a mallet or rolling pin. Layer half of each breast with a slice of ham, followed by cheese. Slice mushrooms thinly and arrange over ham. Cover with the other half of the breasts and seal edges by pounding with the flat end of a knife. Dredge in flour and brown in melted butter. Reduce heat and add a dash or two of the wine. Simmer one minute, add the remainder of the wine and bring back to a simmer. Cook 15 minutes, turning chicken every 5 minutes. Place in a warm oven while making the Balsamella Sauce.

Serves 4

Balsamella Sauce

2 **tablespoons butter**
2 **tablespoons flour**
1 **cup milk**
  Dash of white pepper
¼ **teaspoon salt**

Melt butter over low heat until it begins to froth. Add flour, all at once, and cook, stirring constantly, until flour has expanded and is golden brown. Add milk gradually, stirring constantly. Bring to a boil, stirring constantly; add seasonings and reduce heat. Cook 10 minutes.

Makes 1 cup

Hot Chicken Salad
"It *is* good"

1 cup cooked rice
1 10¾-ounce can cream of
   mushroom soup
¾ cup mayonnaise
1 cup diced celery
1 8-ounce can water
   chestnuts, drained and
   diced
1 cup grated Cheddar
   cheese
½ cup slivered almonds
2 cups diced cooked
   chicken
1 teaspoon dried minced
   onion
½ teaspoon salt
1 cup finely crushed
   potato chips

Combine rice, soup and mayonnaise and mix well. Stir in celery, water chestnuts, cheese, almonds, chicken, onion and salt. Pour in a greased 1½ or 2-quart casserole, top with crushed chips and bake in a 350° oven for 40 to 45 minutes.

Serves 4

Wild Strawberry

Recipes from Wisconsin with Love...

The Hodag was a terrifying creature which reportedly roamed the woods around Rhinelander. It was described as a prehistoric creature with the body of an ox and the tail of an alligator. It had two horns on its head and twelve threatening horns on its back. It breathed fire and had two blinking eyes of unmatching color. In 1896 Gene Shepard captured the Hodag. Some said he used white bulldogs as bait; others said he tied a chloroform-soaked sponge to the end of a 30 foot pole and put the Hodag to sleep in his cave. The monster was in the process of being investigated by scientists from far and wide when it met with untimely destruction. Years later, Shepard finally admitted to constructing the creature himself. But the Hodag had become a local legend, and Rhinelander remains known as the "Home of the Hodag."

Hodag Pie
"Filling enough for a hodag"

1   unbaked pastry shell for a 9-inch pie
1   cup grated Cheddar cheese
2   cups diced cooked chicken or turkey
3   eggs
1/3 cup finely minced onion
1   cup sour cream
1/3 cup mayonnaise
1/2 teaspoon worchestershire sauce
1/4 teaspoon hot pepper sauce
1 1/2 cups chopped fresh broccoli, blanched *

Sprinkle 1/2 cup cheese over bottom of pastry shell. Top with chicken or turkey. Beat eggs; stir in onion, sour cream, mayonnaise, worchestershire and hot pepper sauces. Pour over the cheese and chicken. Sprinkle broccoli on top, followed by the remaining cheese. If desired top with pastry, crimp edges and slit several times. Bake single or double crusted Hodag in 425° oven 30 to 45 minutes or until lightly browned. Let stand at room temperature 10 minutes before serving.

*Frozen chopped broccoli can be substituted for the fresh — just thaw and drain thoroughly before using in the pie.

Makes 1 pie

Recipes from Wisconsin with Love...

The logging boom at the turn of the century brought forth many strong men and tall tales. Paul Bunyan himself had a camp 40 miles from Rhinelander. But this exciting era of Wisconsin's history came to a close when the seemingly inexhaustible pine forests were virtually gone. The Rhinelander Logging Museum preserves the spirit of those days with a reproduction of a logging camp and other logging memorabilia which portray the life of the lumberjack. It has a pair of shoes so enormous it must be Paul Bunyan's! You can also see the famous Hodag at the Logging Museum.

Whiskey Jack was notorious for his feats of strength and endurance while engaged in his occupation of floating lumber rafts down the Wisconsin River. His fame on the river equaled that of Paul Bunyan in the woods. His cook, Big John Marshall, had his hands full feeding Whiskey Jack and his rowdy crew. On the raft, his cooking gear consisted of a frying pan, a kettle and a coffee pot. When asked by Whisky Jack if he ever used a cookbook he replied, "Tried it once, but every recipe started with, 'take a clean dish!'"

Big John's Chicken
"Whiskey Jack's favorite"

1   **chicken, cut in parts**
¼   **cup vegetable oil**
    Flour or commercial biscuit mix
    Seasoned salt
1   **8-ounce box chicken flavored Rice-A-Roni™**

Dredge chicken in flour or biscuit mix. Brown in vegetable oil, seasoning with seasoned salt as desired. Arrange in a slow-cooker or 2-quart casserole. Skim as much oil as possible from the browning skillet, leaving some drippings and all crunchier flour bits. Cook Rice-A-Roni according to package directions in that pan. Pour over chicken and cook in cooker on high setting for 3 to 4 hours or bake in a 350° oven 1 hour.

Serves 4

Mozzarella Chicken and Linguine

3 cloves garlic, crushed
1 tablespoon vegetable oil
1½ to 2 pounds boneless chicken
1 pound linguine
1 16-ounce jar spaghetti sauce
¼ cup hot water
1 4-ounce can sliced mushrooms, drained
¼ teaspoon salt
⅛ teaspoon pepper
4 ounces grated Mozzarella

Sauté garlic in oil; add chicken and brown just 3 minutes per side. Cook linguine according to package instructions, rinse under cold water and drain. Combine spaghetti sauce, water and mushrooms; blend in salt and pepper. Arrange linguine on bottom of a 9 x 13-inch baking dish and pour a third of the sauce on top. Arrange chicken over linguine and cover with remaining sauce. Sprinkle with Mozzarella and bake in a 325° oven 20 to 25 minutes.

Serves 6

Hamlin Garland is one of Wisconsin's most celebrated authors, winning a Pulitzer Prize in 1920. Born in West Salem, the author drew on personal experience and familiar setting to convincingly depict the hardships of the pioneer in his novels of the "Middle Border."

Chicken-Mushroom Casserole

2 cups diced cooked chicken
1 10¾-ounce can cream of mushroom soup
1 10¾-ounce can cream of chicken soup
2 cups cooked egg noodles
1 8-ounce can whole mushrooms, drained
½ cup frozen peas (or drained, canned peas)
1 8-ounce can cream style corn
1 medium onion, chopped
1 cup grated sharp Cheddar cheese
Crumb topping*

Combine chicken and undiluted soups and blend well. Fold in noodles, mushrooms, peas, corn, onion and cheese. Spread into a 9 x 13-inch baking pan or 1½-quart casserole, top with favorite crumb topping and bake 350° oven 35 to 40 minutes or until bubbly and hot. This casserole can be heated in a slow cooker on medium setting for 1½ hours—just omit the crumb topping.

*optional

Serves 4 to 6

A new recipe for duck is always welcome, and we believe that the piquant change of pace provided by zesty Wisconsin cranberries in this one will please your palate. If you especially enjoy duck, keep in mind that the Wild Game Preserve near La Crosse opens for one month of hunting each year.

Duckling with Cranberry Wine Sauce

"Elegant"

2 2½ to 3-pound
  ducklings
1 small onion, quartered
1 celery stalk, sliced
1 carrot, pared and sliced
1 teaspoon salt
1 teaspoon crushed thyme
1 bay leaf
5 cups chicken broth
¼ cup cornstarch
⅔ cup sugar
½ cup dry red wine
1½ cups fresh cranberries

Roast ducks in 475° oven, uncovered, for 15 minutes. Drain off fat, reserving 2 tablespoons, lower temperature to 350° and roast, covered, for 1½ hours. Sauté duck giblets and necks in the reserved fat; add onion, celery, carrot, salt, thyme, bay leaf and broth. Bring to a boil, cover and simmer 1 hour over low heat. Remove ducks to a broiling rack, breast side down, and broil until browned; turn breast side up and repeat broiling until browned. Strain vegetables giblets and neck from the stock. Combine cornstarch and sugar in a saucepan; stir in wine and cranberries. Cook until thick. Stir in 1 cup of strained stock, adjust seasonings if necessary. Serve sauce over ducks.

Serves 4 to 6

Ripon has had a lively political history. A small frame building on the Ripon College campus claims to be the "Birthplace of the Republican Party." In 1854 an anti-slavery group gathered, giving this accounting: "We went into the little meeting Whigs, Free Soilers and Democrats. We came out Republicans and we were the first Republicans in the Union." In 1855 Wisconsin elected a Republican governor and national recognition came to the party at the 1856 convention in Pittsburgh.

Elephant Stew

"A well-known favorite"

1 elephant
50 pounds salt
25 pounds pepper
    Gravy
2 rabbits

Cut elephant into bite sized pieces. This will take about two months. Season with salt and pepper and add enough of your favorite gravy to cover. Cook over low heat 4 weeks. Serves about 3,000 people. If more are expected, add the rabbits. However, do this only if necessary, since most people do not like hares in their stew.

Serves 3,000

Recipes from Wisconsin with Love...

Green Bay is the smallest city in the U.S. to have a major league football team. In addition, the Packers have the distinction of being the only publicly-held team. When it started in 1919, the Indian Packing Company provided its playing field and jerseys, thus the origin of the name. The following hot dish is perfect to serve on a chilly Sunday afternoon, and is so quick and easy it won't interfere with watching the game.

"Packer" Crunch

"For those who packer-it-away"

½ pound ground beef
1 small onion, chopped
½ 10¾-ounce can cream of chicken soup
½ 10¾-ounce can cream of mushroom soup
1¼ cups water
¼ cup uncooked white rice
2 tablespoons soy sauce
Dash of pepper
1 cup chow mein noodles

Brown meat; add onion and cook until tender. Mix together the soups, water, rice, soy sauce and pepper. Stir in meat and pour into a greased 1 or 1½-quart casserole. Bake uncovered in a 350° oven 50 minutes. Sprinkle noodles on top and bake an additional 10 minutes. This casserole can easily be doubled, allowing an extra casserole to be frozen for another meal. To bake the frozen casserole, reduce the oven to 325° and bake an additional 30 minutes.

Serves 2

Recipes from Wisconsin with Love...

The famous author and poet, Carl Sandburg, spent the years from 1907-1912 in Wisconsin. As the state organizer for the Social Democrat Party, he traveled the state with Eugene Debs' "Red Special" presidential campaign train. After he left Wisconsin, he returned to Chicago and pursued his literary career.

"Red Special" Chili Bake

1 **pound ground beef**
1 **16-ounce can whole tomatoes**
1 **17-ounce can kidney beans**
1 **tablespoon chili powder**
½ **teaspoon cumin**
2 **tablespoons dried minced onion**
2 **cups crushed corn chips**
1 **cup grated sharp Cheddar cheese**

Brown beef and drain off excess fat. Add tomatoes, kidney beans, chili powder, cumin and onion. Pour half of this mixture into a 2-quart casserole. Sprinkle with 1 cup corn chips and half of the cheese. Repeat layers. Bake in 350° oven 35 minutes.

Serves 4

Hamburger with Wild Rice
"Nicely seasoned"

5 cups boiling water
1 cup uncooked wild rice
1½ pounds ground beef
⅓ cup chopped onion
¾ cup chopped celery
1 10¾-ounce can cream of mushroom soup
1 10¾-ounce can cream of chicken soup
1 8-ounce can whole mushrooms, drained and sliced
2 beef bouillon cubes
1 bay leaf, crushed
¼ teaspoon celery salt
¼ teaspoon garlic salt
¼ teaspoon onion salt
¼ teaspoon paprika
¼ teaspoon salt*
¼ teaspoon pepper
½ cup slivered almonds

Pour 4 cups boiling water over rice and let stand for 15 to 30 minutes; drain. Meanwhile, brown ground beef, onion and celery. Stir together the undiluted soups and mushrooms. Dissolve bouillon cubes in remaining 1 cup boiling water and blend in with soups. Stir in seasonings. Combine drained rice, browned ground beef mixture and creamed mixture. Pour into a 2-quart casserole, top with almonds, cover and bake in 350° oven 1½ hours.

*Optional

6 to 8 Servings

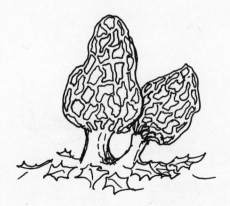

Many of the towns in Wisconsin were settled over 100 years ago by pioneers of European ancestry. They have gone through logging days when towns were crowded Saturday nights with lumberjacks. Railroads have come and gone, as have dozens of small family farms. The complexion of the state has changed through time, but one thing that remains constant is its atmosphere of small town friendliness.

Spaghetti Bake

"Neighborly"

6 ounces spaghetti
1½ pounds ground beef
1 onion chopped
1 tablespoon chili powder
1 16-ounce can cream style corn
1 10¾-ounce can tomato soup
1 10¾-ounce can cream of mushroom soup
8 slices American process cheese food

Cook spaghetti according to package instructions, rinse in cold water and drain. Brown beef with onion; combine with spaghetti, chili powder, corn and soups. Spread in a greased 9 x 13-inch baking pan and arrange cheese slices on top. Bake, covered, in a 350° oven 45 minutes.

Serves 6 to 8

Recipes from Wisconsin with Love...

The "Wisconsin Idea" is a philosophy of government developed by Robert M. LaFollette, Wisconsin's most famous governor and statesman. The first native-born Wisconsin man to become governor, he felt that government should serve the people, rather than rule the people through the power of groups serving their own interests. To pursue this goal, he used advisors from outside the political arena. The "Wisconsin Idea" as developed by LaFollette in the early 1900's has had an impact on politics and social legislation nationwide.

Governor's Hamburger Pie
"Serves the people"

1 pound ground beef
1 egg
1 tablespoon minced onion
1 teaspoon worchestershire sauce
½ teaspoon salt
¼ teaspoon garlic salt
2 cups cooked mixed vegetables
2 cups mashed potatoes

Combine beef, egg, onion, worchestershire, salt and garlic salt; mix well. Press into the bottom of a 9-inch pie pan. Press another 9-inch pie pan firmly over the beef mixture and bake in a 350° oven 10 to 15 minutes. Remove the empty pie pan and bake the ground beef shell an additional 5 minutes. Drain off any excess fat. Fill shell with mixed vegetables and top with mashed potatoes. Bake 20 minutes or until pie is hot.

6 Servings

Spaghetti Pie

6 ounces spaghetti
2 eggs
⅓ cup grated Parmesan cheese
1 cup cottage or Ricotta cheese
1 pound ground beef or pork
½ cup chopped onion
¼ cup chopped green pepper
1 17-ounce can whole tomatoes
1 6-ounce can tomato paste
1 teaspoon sugar
1 teaspoon crushed oregano
½ teaspoon garlic salt
½ cup grated Mozzarella cheese

Snap spaghetti into thirds and cook according to package instructions. Rinse in cold water and drain. Beat eggs and Parmesan cheese together, toss with spaghetti and arrange in the bottom of a greased 9 x 9-inch baking pan. Spread cottage cheese over spaghetti. Brown meat; add onions and green pepper and cook until tender. Stir in undrained tomatoes, tomato paste, sugar, oregano and garlic salt. Bring to a boil, reduce heat and simmer 5 minutes, stirring occasionally to break whole tomatoes into smaller pieces, if desired. Pour mixture over cottage cheese, cover and bake in a 350° oven 20 to 25 minutes. Uncover, sprinkle with Mozzarella and bake 5 minutes longer. Let stand at room temperature 10 minutes before serving.

Serves 4

Recipes from Wisconsin with Love . . .

In Milwaukee harbor is a point of land that once was an island. Jones Island attracted a Squatter's Settlement after the Civil War, with a population that once exceeded 3000. It became an island unto itself, for years maintaining its own informal government and law enforcement under the leadership of a Polish fisherman named Jacob Muzo. It is said that during that time the Milwaukee police did not dare venture onto the island. In 1914, however, the city bought the island and began developing it as a harbor. The last squatter lingered until 1943.

Squatter's Chili

1 **pound ground beef, or cubed round steak**
3 **large onions, chopped**
2 **ribs celery, chopped**
1 **28-ounce can peeled chunk tomatoes**
1 **12-ounce can tomato paste**
3 **large green peppers, chopped**
1 **12-ounce can beer**
2 **tablespoons chili powder**
2 **tablespoons cumin**
2 **16-ounce cans dark red kidney beans**
1 **16-ounce can hot chili pinto beans**

Brown meat with onions and celery. Add green peppers, tomatoes, tomato paste, beer and seasonings, stirring to blend well. Simmer 45 minutes. Add undrained beans and simmer an additional 15 to 20 minutes. If desired, top with grated Cheddar cheese, chopped raw onion or oyster crackers when serving.

Serves 4 to 6

This is originally a Pennsylvania Dutch recipe, transplanted to Wisconsin by a family of modern-day pioneers. This recipe has been in the family for many generations and has changed little since the family left their Pennsylvania farm 50 years ago to move to Beloit. Hearty and satisfying, this dish was always served in the fall, at harvest time, when the hog was slaughtered for the coming winter. It was then that the maw, or stomach, of the pig was available. Originally, the frugal farmers mixed the ingredients and stuffed them into the maw, the thick football-shaped covering which imparted its own special flavor when baked to a golden brown. The mixture was then removed and eaten with fresh bread and butter. Cooked as a casserole, it's still a great dish.

Hog Maw
"Pennsylvania Dutch"

6 large potatoes, diced
½ pound lean ground pork
2½ pounds pork sausage without casing
2 pounds lean ground beef
1 large cabbage, chopped
3 large onions, chopped
2 tablespoons salt
1 teaspoon pepper
2 tablespoons parsley flakes
1 teaspoon garlic powder
1 teaspoon caraway seeds*
1 teaspoon crushed hot red peppers*

Cook potatoes in boiling water for 5 minutes. Drain. Combine with remaining ingredients and mix well. Spread into a 3-quart casserole and bake in 350° oven 2½ hours. Mixture may alternatively be stuffed into a pig's stomach and baked at 350° for 3 hours.

*optional

Serves 8

Recipes from Wisconsin with Love...

Summerfest in Milwaukee offers a keyhole view into cosmopolitan life and a sampling of small neighborhoods. For eleven days the best in talent, food, music and entertainment is offered in a lakefront setting. This is followed by seven weekends at the festival grounds featuring Italian, German, Afro, Mexican, Irish, Polish and finally the Music Festival. Golubtsi is a Slavic dish you might find served at one of the ethnic fests.

Golubtsi
"Stuffed cabbage leaves"

1 **pound ground beef**
2 **cups cooked rice**
¼ **cup chopped onion**
1 **teaspoon salt**
½ **teaspoon pepper**
1 **medium to large head cabbage**

Broth:
1 **16-ounce can tomatoes**
¼ **cup chopped onion**
2 **cloves garlic, minced or pressed**
½ **teaspoon salt**
¼ **teaspoon pepper**

Combine ground beef, rice, onion, salt and pepper. Steam or blanch cabbage just long enough to soften the leaves. (You'll need at least a dozen.) Put about ¼-cup ground beef mixture in center of each leaf; fold each side over. Place seam side down in a 3-quart kettle, making three or four layers. Make broth by combining the undrained tomatoes with enough water to make 6 cups. Add onion, garlic, salt and pepper; blend well and pour over the stuffed leaves. Bring to a boil, reduce heat to create a slow boil, cover and cook 30 to 40 minutes. Serve in bowls with sour cream. Excess broth can be refrigerated and incorporated into other casseroles, if desired.

Serves 4

Recipes from Wisconsin with Love..

Scandinavians are the second largest ethnic population in Wisconsin. This recipe was brought over from Sweden, and has been passed on for four generations. A tried and true recipe!

Swedish Meat Balls

¼ cup butter
⅓ cup minced onion
1 egg
½ cup milk
½ cup bread crumbs
1¼ teaspoons salt
2 teaspoons sugar
½ teaspoon allspice
¼ teaspoon nutmeg
1 pound ground beef
¼ pound ground pork
1 cup water

Melt 2 tablespoons butter; add onion and sauté until golden. In mixing bowl, beat egg; stir in milk and crumbs. Set aside 5 minutes. Combine bread crumb mixture with sautéed onion, salt, sugar, allspice and nutmeg. Stir in ground meats and blend well. Shape into 1½-inch balls and brown in remaining 2 tablespoons butter. Pour in water and simmer 20 minutes.

6 Servings

At the outset, let us reassure you this is not a recipe for feeding Great Danes. Nor does the recipe call for a Great Dane in its ingredients. However, it is a great Danish recipe! And you'll probably find it on the menu in the cafes of Racine, a community that boasts one of the largest Danish populations in the U.S.

Great Danish Goulash

1 pound round steak
3 tablespoons olive oil
   Dash of pepper
¾ cup thinly sliced onion
2 teaspoons salt
   Cold water
1 tablespoon brown sugar
3 small bay leaves
3 tablespoons flour

Cut meat in cubes and brown in oil seasoned with pepper. Add onions and sauté until light brown. Add salt, 2½ cups water, brown sugar and bay leaves; simmer, covered, for 1½ hours or until tender. Remove bay leaves. Combine flour and 5 tablespoons water, blending until smooth. Gradually add to meat, stirring constantly, and cook until sauce is smooth and thickened. Serve over rice or buttered noodles. This recipe can easily be tripled for larger groups and made a day ahead. Just bring to serving temperature before serving.

4 Servings

A cornish miner liked his pasty to "stand up" to working conditions. Miners were lowered by windlass some 40-50 feet down a shaft into the black tunnels which meandered for miles underground. Many of the towns of southwestern Wisconsin are built on top of these subterranean passageways. His job being as it was, a miner could not afford frailty in any respect, so a good pasty was one that could be dropped down these deep shafts and not break apart, even if they hit the bottom.

Cornish Pasty

1 Unbaked pastry for a double-crust 10-inch pie
2 pounds sirloin, cut in ½-inch chunks
2 medium potatoes, pared and sliced
3 medium onions, chopped
½ cup diced suet
½ teaspoon salt
¼ teaspoon pepper
¼ cup whipping cream

Roll two-thirds of pastry to fit bottom of a 10-inch pie pan. Mix meat, potatoes, onions, suet and seasonings and arrange in the pastry. Roll out remaining pastry, fit over meat, crimp pastry edges together and slit the top. Bake in preheated 400° oven 20 minutes; reduce temperature to 350° and bake an additional 1½ hours. Pour cream through slits and return to oven for 15 more minutes.

Makes 1 pie

Lumber laid the foundations for Eau Claire, also known as the "Sawdust City." Here, where the Chippewa and Eau Claire Rivers meet, millions of logs came crashing down the rivers every spring. They were caught and held at Beef Slough, the name given to the network of waterways which constituted one of the biggest log harbors in Wisconsin.

Beef Slough Stew
"Brothy"

2 pounds cubed or chunked beef
2 tablespoons vegetable oil
4 cups boiling water
1 teaspoon lemon juice
1 teaspoon worchestershire sauce
1 clove garlic, minced
1 medium onion, chopped
1 clove whole garlic
2 bay leaves
1 teaspoon salt
½ teaspoon pepper
½ teaspoon paprika
Dash of allspice
Dash of cloves
1 teaspoon sugar
8 medium potatoes, pared and diced
4 carrots, pared and thickly sliced
2 medium onions, quartered

Brown beef in oil in a large Dutch oven or kettle. Add water, lemon juice, worchestershire, minced garlic, chopped onion, whole garlic, bay leaves, salt, pepper, paprika, allspice, cloves and sugar. Cover and cook over medium heat 1 hour. Add potatoes, carrots and quartered onions; cook an additional 30 minutes. Remove bay leaves before serving.

Serves 6

When lead was unearthed in Wisconsin in the 1820's, it attracted two kinds of new settlers. The "Suckers" were those who came from other states for the summer and returned to their cozy homes when the weather turned cold. The tenacious miners who stayed in Wisconsin through the winters and dug their homes into the hillsides or lived in caves to survive were known as "Badgers." Their perseverence was instrumental in Wisconsin's growth to territorial status, and in endowing Wisconsin with its nickname "The Badger State."

Badger Stew

"Your family will badger you for more"

3	pounds cubed or chunked beef
½	cup flour
3	tablespoons vegetable oil
3	cups chopped onion
1	pound carrots, pared and thickly sliced
4	cloves garlic, minced or crushed
3	cups beef stock or broth
1½	teaspoons fine herbs
1	12-ounce can beer
2	bay leaves
¼	teaspoon pepper
½	teaspoon salt
1	cup water

Coat beef cubes in flour; heat oil in large Dutch casserole, add meat and brown. Add onion, carrots, garlic, beef stock, beer, bay leaves, herbs, salt and pepper. Bring mixture to a boil, reduce heat and simmer, covered, 1½ hours or until meat is tender. Add water as necessary during the cooking process. Remove bay leaves before serving. This stew is great served over baked potatoes.

Serves 8

The overview of LaCrosse from Grandad Bluff makes it clear why this is called "God's Country." Three converging rivers make this the most strategic Mississippi River port, earning it the title of "Gateway City." The three rivers, the Mississippi, the LaCrosse and the Black provided canoe access for the Indians who once gathered on this neutral ground to compete in the sport which gave LaCrosse its name. As a reminder of the hundreds of paddleboats that once occupied the waterways, the impressive double-decked LaCrosse Queen still docks at Riverside Park, which is also the home of the new "Riverside USA." This picturesque sight greets thousands of visitors each year to the nationally recognized Oktoberfest, a high-spirited celebration of LaCrosse's strong German culture.

Rouladin

"Very German"

1 **pound flank or round steak**
4 **carrots, pared and sliced lengthwise**
3 **stalks celery, sliced lengthwise**
4 **large dill pickle spears, sliced lengthwise**
¼ **to ½ teaspoon salt**
⅛ **to ¼ teaspoon pepper Flour**
¼ **cup vegetable oil**
½ **cup dry red wine**
½ **cup water**
10 **ginger snaps, crushed***
4 **tablespoons water**

Pound steak to about ½" thick. Arrange carrots, celery and pickles across meat; roll up as for a jelly roll and tie with string. Sprinkle with salt and pepper, dredge in flour and brown in hot oil, turning frequently. Add wine and water to the skillet and simmer, covered, 1 hour, turning meat occasionally. Remove meat to a platter and cut string off. Thicken pan juices with the ginger snaps and serve with meat.

*2 tablespoons cornstarch blended into ¼ cup water can be substituted.

Serves 4

Recipes from Wisconsin with Love...

Cedar Creek Settlement in Cedarburg is a restoration of the historic village that revolved around the Wittenberg Woolen Mills. The original mill building and dam were built completely by hand in 1864. Business boomed during the Civil War as power from the dam ran the looms and knitting machines which filled the demands for heavy woolens on the front. The restoration also includes the covered bridge, flour mill and winery. Several of the buildings in this pioneer settlement are on the National Register of Historic Places.

Roast Beef and Yorkshire Pudding

"Yorkshire pudding is similar to a popover, except baked in the roast beef drippings"

5 pounds sirloin roast
rubbed with salt and
pepper
1 cup flour
1/2 teaspoon salt
1 cup milk
2 eggs

Roast meat to desired doneness on rack in roasting pan in 325° oven. (Do not add water.) Transfer meat to platter and keep warm. Pour 1/4 cup of roast drippings into a preheated 11 x 7 1/2-inch baking pan or dish. Combine flour, salt and milk and beat until smooth. Add eggs, one at a time, beating just until blended after each addition. Pour batter into pan and bake 25 minutes, until puffed and golden. Cut into squares and serve with carved beef.

Serves 8

Veal Parmesan

1 egg
1 cup dry whole wheat bread crumbs
⅓ cup wheat germ
½ cup grated Parmesan cheese
4 cubed veal cutlets
1 tablespoon vegetable oil
4 slices Mozzarella cheese
1 15-ounce can spaghetti sauce

Beat egg and pour into a flat dish or plate. Combine bread crumbs, wheat germ and ¼ cup of the Parmesan cheese. Dip each cutlet into the egg, then into the crumbs. Coat well. Heat oil and brown cutlets. Arrange in a large, flat baking dish and top each with a slice of Mozzarella. Pour sauce over casserole and sprinkle with the remaining Parmesan cheese. Cover and bake in a preheated 325° oven 45 to 50 minutes or until meat is tender.

4 Servings

Recipes from Wisconsin with Love...

The Huntsinger Farms outside Eau Claire is the world's largest grower and producer of that racy-tasting long stringy root—horseradish. Ellis Huntsinger, a German who enjoyed his horseradish as much as any, did get tired of grating it every meal. One morning, he accidentally spilled cream into his fish bowl of fresh horseradish, and at noon it was still "hot." This led to the creation of horesradish sauces which can spark the flavors of many meats, fishes and vegetables, as this recipe proves.

Corned Beef with Horseradish Sauce

3 pounds corned beef brisket
Dash of garlic salt
Dash of celery salt
1 tablespoon brown sugar
1½ pounds new potatoes (or 2 1-pound cans whole Irish potatoes)
1½ pounds carrots, pared and cut in 2-inch chunks
1 large head cabbage, cut in 6 wedges
2 chicken bouillon cubes
Salt

Horseradish Sauce:
1½ cups vegetable stock
4 chicken bouillon cubes
1 tablespoon sugar
Dash of white pepper
¼ cup butter
2 tablespoons flour
1 cup whipping cream
Dash of nutmeg
1½ tablespoons horseradish

Serves 6 to 8

Sprinkle meat with garlic and celery salts; rub brown sugar into non-fatty sides. Roast, fatty side up, about 3 hours in 350° oven. Bring one gallon of water to boil in large (2 gallon) kettle at least 40 minutes before eating. Add bouillon cubes and salt, if desired. Add raw potatoes, boil 15 minutes, add carrots and cook another 10 minutes. Add cabbage and cook just 10 minutes more. Remove 1½ cups stock for the sauce. To make sauce, dissolve the bouillon cubes in the 1½ cups stock; add sugar and pepper and bring to a boil. In a small saucepan, melt butter, skim half off and discard. Stir flour into the remaining melted butter and cook until the mixture begins to expand. With wire whisk, whip half of this flour mixture into the 1½ cups boiling stock. Gradually whip in cream. Finally, whip in the remaining flour mixture, bring sauce to a boil, stirring constantly, and add nutmeg. Stir in horseradish, beggining with 1 tablespoon and adding more to taste. To serve, drain vegetables, carve meat and arrange on platter. Accompany with the sauce.

Recipes from Wisconsin with Love...

Wisconsin has a rich Indian heritage. The Ojibwe, or Chippewa, were great hunters and gatherers, and were equally adept at making good use of the bounties of nature. This hearty stew is a creative and appetizing alternative to deer sausage.

Venison Stew

2 pounds cubed or chunked lean venison
1 teaspoon salt
1 teaspoon vinegar
5 tablespoons lard
3 pounds carrots, pared and sliced
3 large potatoes, pared and diced
1 large onion, sliced
4 cloves garlic
2 bay leaves
1/8 teaspoon rosemary
1/2 teaspoon cumin
6 whole allspice

Soak meat overnight with salt and vinegar in enough water to cover. The next day, drain and rinse the meat; boil 5 minutes in 2 or 3 cups water. Drain and brown meat in lard. In a large pot combine the meat, vegetables and seasonings. Pour in enough water to cover and bring to a boil. Boil 40 minutes or until meat is tender. Remove bay leaves before serving.

Serves 6

Recipes from Wisconsin with Love.

Fried Rice Deluxe

2 **cups uncooked rice**
5 **cups water**
2 **chicken bouillon cubes**
1 **cup julienned or diced pork, chicken, beef or shrimp**
2 **tablespoons soy sauce**
2 **teaspoons pepper**
¼ **cup vegetable oil**
2 **cloves garlic, minced**
2 **tablespoons baby green peas**
2 **eggs**

Bring rice to boil in water seasoned with bouillon cubes. Cook 30 to 40 minutes or until rice is done. Drain and cool. Toss meat with 1 tablespoon soy sauce and 1 teaspoon pepper. Sauté garlic in hot oil; add meat and stir fry until meat is nearly done. Add peas and rice; continue to stir fry until well mixed. Make a well in the middle of the rice. Beat eggs slightly and pour into well; stir lightly. Combine with rice and meat when eggs are cooked. Toss rice with remaining soy sauce and pepper before serving.

Serves 4

Bloodroot

The House on the Rock is Wisconsin's #1 privately-owned tourist attraction. Looming atop the 60-foot high Deershelter Rock, it was originally hand-built as a summer home by Alex Jordan. Now a fantastic collection, it includes the original house, a gate house, a mill house with guns, dolls, antique music machines, a nostalgic Street of Yesteryear, a 35-foot doll house, the world's largest carousel, a 45-foot perpetual motion clock, a 56-foot giant cannon, a roomful of automated one-of-a-kind music machines with life-like characters including "The Mikado," and more and more. This amazing spectacle is located between Spring Green and Dodgeville.

Pork Mikado

2½ pounds lean pork, cut in
  2-inch chunks
¼ cup soy sauce
¼ cup vegetable oil
4 chicken bouillon cubes
2 cups boiling water

1 20-ounce can
  unsweetened
  pineapple chunks
½ cup sugar
⅓ cup cider vinegar
¼ cup cornstarch
3 tablespoons cold water
2 green peppers, seeded
  and coarsely chopped

Combine pork and soy sauce, mixing or tossing to coat evenly. Heat oil and add pork; brown. Reduce heat and simmer 20 minutes, stirring occasionally. In a small saucepan, dissolve bouillon cubes in boiling water. Drain pineapples, pouring liquid into the bouillon. Set pineapple chunks aside. Stir sugar and vinegar into the bouillon; pour mixture over simmering pork. Cover and simmer 30 minutes or until meat is tender. Blend cornstarch and cold water into a paste; add to simmering pork, stirring constantly, until gravy thickens. Boil 3 minutes. Stir in pineapple and green pepper; cook 5 minutes or until peppers are just tender. Serve over rice.

Serves 4 to 6

Baked Pork Chops Creole
"A jazzy blend of flavors"

4 **pork chops**
2 **tablespoons vegetable oil**
¾ **cup uncooked brown rice**
2 **large tomatoes**
1 **large onion**
½ **green pepper**
½ **teaspoon salt**
⅛ **teaspoon freshly ground pepper**
⅛ **teaspoon thyme**
⅛ **teaspoon marjoram or oregano**
1½ **cups chicken broth**

Brown chops in oil. Pour rice in a greased 9 x 9-inch baking pan and arrange chops on top. Slice tomatoes into 8 rings, onions into 4 rings and green pepper into 4 rings. Arrange vegetables over chops. Sprinkle seasonings on top and pour broth over casserole. Cover and bake in a preheated 350° oven 1 hour or until rice is tender and chops are done.

4 Servings

In 1950 there were about a million cherry trees in Door County and this region is still known for its wonderfully tart cherries. Sturgeon Bay is the host of Cherry Blossom Week in May. Although most of the cherries canned from the harvest go into pies, they can also be used to great advantage in the following cherry sauce.

Baked Ham with Cherry Sauce

1 fully cooked, semi-boneless 6-pound ham
1 16-ounce can tart red cherries
½ cup plus 1½ tablespoons water
1½ cups sugar
1½ tablespoons cornstarch
Dash of salt
1 tablespoon brandy*

Bake ham in 300° oven 1½ hours. Meanwhile, drain cherries, pouring juice into a saucepan; set cherries aside. Add ½ cup water and sugar to juice; bring to a boil. Blend cornstarch with 1½ tablespoons water and stir into boiling juice. Add salt and reserved cherries; bring back to a boil. Remove from heat, stir in brandy and serve over ham.

*optional

Serves 6 to 8

Recipes from Wisconsin with Love...

Mushroom and Ham Lasagna

1 **8-ounce package lasagna noodles**
2 **cups ricotta cheese**
¼ **cup milk**
½ **teaspoon salt**
⅛ **teaspoon freshly ground pepper**
1 **4-ounce can mushroom stems and pieces, drained**
½ **cup chopped green onions**
2 **tablespoons butter**
1 **15-ounce can whole tomatoes**
1 **cup cubed cured ham**
2 **tablespoons snipped parsley**
2 **tablespoons dry white wine**
½ **teaspoon crushed dried basil**
1 **cup grated fontinella cheese**
1 **pound Garlic Jack or sharp Cheddar cheese, sliced thinly**

Cook noodles according to package instructions, rinse in cold water and drain. Combine ricotta, milk, salt and pepper. Sauté mushrooms and onion in butter just until tender. Drain tomatoes, reserving liquid, and quarter; stir into sautéed vegetables with parsley, wine, basil and half the reserved tomato liquid. Simmer 5 to 8 minutes or until liquid is almost evaporated. Arrange a single layer of noodles in bottom of a greased 9 x 9-inch baking dish. Spread one-third of the cheese mixture over the noodles, followed by a third of the tomato mixture, a third of the sliced cheese and a third of the fontinella. Repeat layers in order twice. Cover with foil and bake in 350° oven 35 to 40 minutes. Cool 10 minutes at room temperature before serving. This recipe can be doubled so that a batch can be frozen—just bake the frozen lasagna in a 325° oven for 1 to 1¼ hours.

Serves 4 to 6

Promotional advertising helped populate Sheboygan. It was common for Germans in the Old Country to gather on street corners and around kitchen tables to examine the delights of Wisconsin via letters and promotional pamphlets. The more adventurous packed their family and belongings under the motivation of the printed promises of this land of opportunity. An industrial city, Sheboygan is also celebrated for its sausages.

Sheboygan Brats

6 to 8 bratwurst
1 large onion, chopped
2 12-ounce cans beer
1 16- ounce can
    sauerkraut

Grill brats over slow coals until golden brown, turning often. Meanwhile, combine onion and beer in a large pot and set on grill to heat. Place grilled brats in beer and simmer 10 to 20 minutes. Heat sauerkraut and serve alongside brats.

6 to 8 Servings

Recipes from Wisconsin with Love...

The worst lies are the most enthusiastically applauded at the annual tall-tale competition of the Liar's Club. Headquartered in Burlington, the Liar's Club was started "to preserve a little bit of Americana which vanished with the old-time grocery store when our grandads used to gather and spin their wonderfully concocted yarns."

Wurst-Beer Salad

"The best around"

⅓ cup beer
3 tablespoons olive oil
3 tablespoons vinegar
⅛ teaspoon dill weed
⅛ teaspoon dry mustard
⅛ teaspoon crushed thyme
¼ teaspoon crushed basil
1 tablespoon minced parsley
1 clove garlic, minced or pressed
Salt
Pepper
2 to 4 potatoes, cooked, peeled and sliced
½ large red onion, chopped
½ pound knockwurst, cooked and sliced

Combine beer, olive oil, vinegar, seasonings and herbs in a pint jar; cover and shake well. Combine potatoes, onion and knockwurst. Pour dressing over the meat and potatoes, toss and chill at least 1 hour before serving

Serves 2

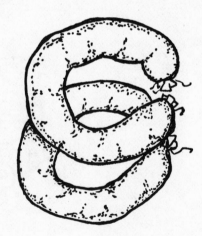

Recipes from Wisconsin with Love...

Much of the sauerkraut associated with Wisconsin and its large German population is produced from cabbage grown in the Sturtevant area. During World War II, when anti-German feelings were high, sauerkraut was called "liberty cabbage."

Sausage and Liberty Cabbage

2 tablespoons vegetable oil
3 pounds smoked or Polish sausage
2 large potatoes, diced
2 large apples, pared and diced
1 teaspoon garlic salt
¼ teaspoon salt
⅛ teaspoon pepper
1 32-ounce can sauerkraut
1 12-ounce can beer

Heat oil in oven-proof skillet and brown sausages; add potatoes and brown. Stir in apples and simmer several minutes. Sprinkle with seasonings and arrange sauerkraut on top; simmer several minutes. Pour beer over sauerkraut, cover and bake in a 350° oven 45 minutes.

Serves 6 to 8

The area around Winter is noted for its excellent musky waters. Wisconsin's State Fish, the muskellunge can reach over five feet in length and weigh more than 70 pounds. It's a highly prized game fish, not only for its size, but also because of its ferocious and obstinate fighting spirit. Fishermen have a scientific obsession with trying to outsmart the big one. But this fish is often misunderstood when it finally reaches the kitchen. Here is a recipe to increase your musky savvy.

Husky Musky
"Tames your prize catch"

1 **5 to 7-pound skinned**
musky fillet
Salted water
6 **or 7 peppercorns**
½ **teaspoon caraway seeds**

Place fillet in a large pot with enough lightly salted water to completely cover. Place peppercorns and caraway seeds in a tea ball or cheesecloth pouch and place in fish pot. Bring water to a boil, reduce heat and simmer just until fish is white and flaky. Cooking time will vary—do not overcook. Drain and serve in chunks accompanied with melted butter for dipping into.

Serves 6

MUSKELLUNGE
Esox masquinongy masquinongy

Credit goes to Paul Bunyan for Wisconsin's numerous inland lakes. When he jumped from the top of Rib Mountain, near Eau Claire, into the Wisconsin River, he created a splash so huge that each drop created a lake where it landed. We suspect that Paul got his amazing pet fish from one of these lakes. It learned how to walk and accompanied Paul everywhere. Alas, the fish fell into one of the lakes one day, and by that time had forgotten how to swim, and it drowned. As the fish would have had it, Paul deliciously deep-fried his faithful pet, and it served its master once again.

Paul Bunyan's Fish
"Deep-fried freshwater fish"

½ cup beer
½ cup water
   Dash of cayenne
   Dash of nutmeg
   Dash of garlic salt
¾ cup flour
¼ cup cornstarch
8 whitefish fillets or 20 jumbo shrimp
   Vegetable oil

Combine beer, water, seasonings, flour and cornstarch; beat well. Pat fillets dry with paper toweling and coat in batter. Deep fry in oil heated to 375° until golden brown.

Hints for deep-frying: Fish will be crispier if coated in batter immediately before placing in the fryer. Therefore, don't coat all the fish at once-only the amount you'll be frying. Also, fish shouldn't be dropped in the oil—use tongs to immerse fish in oil for several seconds before releasing.

Serves 3 to 4

Outdoor fish boils give Door County a special flavor and aroma. This is an event loved by visitors as well as the local folk. Delicious freshly-caught fish and a dramatic grand finale in the preparation make this a gratifying group-participation project, both in the making and in the eating.

Door County Outdoor Fish Boil

20 **medium to large**
potatoes
Several whole onions,
peeled
2 **cups salt**
10 **pounds whitefish or**
trout fillets, chunked

Equipment needed:
A huge bucket
A wire basket to fit
inside the bucket
An open fire
A cup of fuel oil or
kerosene (not gasoline)

Scrub potatoes, leaving skins on; place in the bottom of the bucket, add the onions and cover with water to three-fourths full. Bring to a boil over the fire. Add a cup of salt and boil vigorously for 20 minutes. Place fish chunks in the wire basket and submerge into bucket with the potatoes. If necessary, stoke the fire to bring water back to boil. Add the additional cup of salt and boil 5 minutes. Now the drama: Gather the people together for the "boil-over." Take your fuel oil and carefully throw it on the fire. The water will boil furiously and overflow from the kettle, removing the scum. Take the bucket from the fire, remove the basket and arrange fish on a platter. Drain the potatoes and onions and serve wtih lots of butter. Homemade bread, a salad or slaw and, of course, cherry pie makes this a real Door County treat.

Serves 20

For those who love that "out-Door County" spirit but are limited by uncooperative weather or the lack of a back yard, this recipe is adapted for the kitchen. The added vegetables make it a full meal in a pot. Savored indoors or out, this nutritious and colorful dish will impart that festive Door County feeling.

Door County Indoor Fish Boil
"Adapted for indoor cooking"

10 cups water
⅓ cup salt
12 small potatoes
6 medium onions
1 head cabbage, cut in 6 wedges
2 pounds whitefish fillets, cut in chunks
1 16-ounce can small whole beets
Parsley, finely minced

Horseradish Sauce:
½ cup horseradish
1 tablespoon flour
¼ teaspoon paprika
½ teaspoon salt
1 cup half-and-half

Bring water to a boil in a large kettle and add salt. Pare a strip of skin from the middle of each potato; add to water with onions and simmer 30 minutes or until tender. Add cabbage and simmer another 10 minutes. Add fish and simmer 3 to 4 minutes or just until fish is flaky. Remove vegetables and fish to a serving platter and keep warm. Heat beets in water; remove to platter. Pour horseradish sauce over vegetables and fish and garnish with parsley to serve. To make sauce, combine horseradish, flour, paprika and salt in a small saucepan. Stir in half-and-half. Cook, stirring constantly, until thickened.

Serves 6

The Brule River in northwestern Wisconsin is much acclaimed for its superb trout fishing. Among its credentials is an endorsement by President Coolidge who, following a three-month sojourn in Brule, pronounced: "The fishing around here, I can testify, is very excellent." Flash your fish proficiency with this delicious two-fish dish.

Molded Trout and Salmon with Herbed Hollandise
"Elegant"

10 ¼-pound trout fillets
2 tablespoons egg whites
1 cup whipping cream
2 tablespoons minced fresh parsley
2 tablespoons snipped fresh chives

¼ teaspoon white pepper
½ teaspoon salt
8 ounces flaked canned salmon
¼ cup melted butter

Cut two of the fillets into 1-inch pieces; cover with boiling water and simmer 10 minutes, until tender. Drain, flake, and chill. Lightly beat 1 tablespoon egg white; combine with ⅓ cup cream, parsley, chives, ⅛ teaspoon white pepper and ¼ teaspoon salt. Stir in chilled trout flakes, blend well and cover. Refrigerate 1 hour. Meanwhile, combine salmon, remaining tablespoon egg white, lightly beaten, and the remaining cream, salt and pepper. Blend well, cover and refrigerate 1 hour. When ready to assemble and bake, place the remaining 8 trout fillets between sheets of waxed paper and flatten slightly with a mallet or rolling pin. Thoroughly butter an oven-proof mold or casserole and arrange the fillets on the bottom and sides. Cover and refrigerate 30 minutes. Spoon the flaked trout mixture over the fillets, smoothing to make an even layer. Spoon the salmon mixture on top, smoothing again to make an even layer. Fold ends of the fillets over the salmon (there should be enough to cover). Cover with buttered waxed paper and a double layer of aluminum foil and place inside a large pan or Dutch oven. Add enough hot water to submerge half of the mold. Bake in a 350° oven 50 minutes or until a knife inserted in center comes out clean. Cool 10 minutes, drain off excess liquid and invert onto a heated platter. Pat dry with paper towels and brush with melted butter. Decorate with parsley, cucumber slices, radish slices or any other garnish. Serve with herbed hollandaise.

Serves 6 to 8

Herbed Hollandaise Sauce

2 to 4 teaspoons lemon
  juice
1 tablespoon minced fresh
  chives
2 teaspoons minced green
  onion
1 tablespoon minced
  parsley

2 tablespoons hot water
2 tablespoons distilled
  white vinegar
¼ teaspoon salt
  Dash of white pepper
1 tablespoon cold water
3 egg yolks
1 cup unsalted butter

Combine hot water, vinegar, salt and white pepper; bring to a boil and boil until liquid is reduced to 2 tablespoons. Remove from heat and stir in cold water. Beat egg yolks lightly and gradually add to vinegar mixture, stirring constantly. Cook over low heat, stirring constantly until thick. Add butter, one tablespoon at a time, stirring until butter melts after each addition. Blend in lemon juice. Remove from heat and place pan in a large bowl of warm water. Stir in the chives, green onion and parsley. Just before serving, pour sauce into a heated gravy boat or over the food it accompanies.

Makes about 1½ cups

Recipes from Wisconsin with Love...

Along the Mississippi River in the southern part of the state, small towns appear to be climbing up the rocks. The buildings are wedged in between the river and the bluffs. In fact, the town of Potosi is said to have the longest main street in the world—with no intersecting streets. The river shore often presents the tranquil scene of people fishing, probably for catfish. They are patiently anticipating that 70-pound prize, undaunted by the fact that it might look like a half-grown pig.

Mississippi Catfish
"Tastes better with batter"

1½ cups corn meal
1 tablespoon garlic salt
½ teaspoon cayenne
½ teaspoon pepper
3 eggs
1½ cups milk
1 teaspoon lemon juice
12 6-ounce catfish fillets
Butter

Combine corn meal, garlic salt, cayenne and pepper. Beat eggs, milk and lemon juice. Pat fillets dry with paper toweling. Dip each fillet first in the egg mixture, then in the corn meal mixture, coating well. Sauté in hot melted butter until golden brown. Serve with lemon wedges and tartar sauce.

12 servings

Tartar Sauce

1 cup mayonnaise
2 tablespoons chopped dill pickle
1 tablespoon minced onion
1 tablespoon minced parsley
2 teaspoons white vinegar
1 teaspoon sugar
2 teaspoons pimiento*
½ teaspoon hot pepper sauce*

Combine all ingredients and blend well. Cover and refrigerate until ready to serve.

*optional

Makes 1½ cups

Every fisherman has a story about the big one that got away. At the National Fresh Water Fishing Hall of Fame in Hayward, you can make history with that once-in-a-lifetime catch in the "One That Didn't Get Away Department."

Hall of Fame Broiled Fish

1 **pound whitefish fillets**
4 **tablespoons melted butter**
  Salt
  Paprika
¼ **cup blanched almond halves**
1 **tablespoon lemon juice**
  Parsley

Brush fillets with 2 tablespoons melted butter and broil, without turning, 3 to 4 inches from flame until just cooked. Arrange on a platter and season with salt and paprika. Sauté almonds in remaining 2 tablespoons butter, stir in lemon juice and spoon over fillets. Garnish with minced parsley, if desired, and serve.

Serves 3

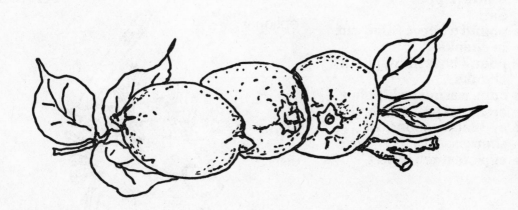

Some of the best fresh-water fishing in the world is found in Wisconsin's two great lakes, 15,000 inland lakes and about 2400 streams and rivers. These bounteous waters give the serious fisherman and the idle dangler alike a rewarding opportunity to go for the catch of choice or to take pot-luck. The following chowder recipe is great as written, or with any fish you catch added in or substituted.

Fish Chowder

"Chow-down chowder"

1¼ **cups melted butter**
3 **tablespoons flour**
2 **cups fish stock**
1 **or 2 medium potatoes, diced**
1 **or 2 stalks celery, diced**
1 **or 2 medium carrots, pared and diced**
1 **medium onion, chopped**
 Dash of nutmeg
 Dash of thyme
 White pepper
 Salt
½ **pound walleye fillet, cut in chunks**
½ **pound bass fillet, cut in chunks**
4 **cups warmed whipping cream or half-and-half**
2 **or 3 tablespoons dry sherry**
¼ **cup creamed butter** *

Combine flour and melted butter; beat well and set aside. Bring fish stock to boil over medium heat in a 2-quart saucepan. Add potatoes, celery, carrots, onion, nutmeg, thyme, and pepper and salt as desired; bring back to a boil, cover and cook 15 minutes or until vegetables are tender. Add fish and simmer 10 minutes more. Gradually add flour and butter mixture, stirring constantly, and cook 5 minutes. Blend in cream and sherry and bring to a boil; remove from heat and add creamed butter and more salt and pepper, if needed.

Serves 8

*optional

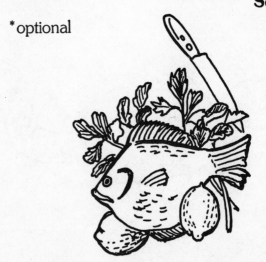

The S.S. Meteor is the last remaining whaleback freighter. It was launched in 1896 and was used to haul iron ore. It is now harbored on Barker's Island in Superior, and serves as a maritime museum.

Seafood Hotdish

2 cups cooked rice
1 3-ounce can baby shrimp, rinsed and drained*
1 3-ounce can flaked crab*
1 cup whipping cream
¼ cup melted butter
1½ teaspoons hot pepper sauce
1 tablespoon worchestershire sauce
1 cup finely crushed potato chips

Combine rice, seafood, cream, butter and sauces. Pour into a greased 1 or 1½-quart casserole and top with crushed chips. Bake in a 300° oven 25 to 30 minutes.

*An 8-ounce package of frozen snowflake crab with baby shrimp can be substituted for the canned — just thaw and drain before mixing with the other ingredients.

Serves 4

Recipes from Wisconsin with Love...

Porte des Morts, the half-mile strait between Door Peninsula and Washington Island, is one of the most treacherous stretches of water on Lake Michigan. Hundreds of shipwrecks are reported to have happened there. The Griffin, one of the first sailing vessels on the Great Lakes, met with devastation in 1679. But the Griffin, or its ghost, is still seen riding the waves at "Death's Door."

Windjammer Shrimp
"Right on course"

¼ cup butter
1½ teaspoons curry powder
½ cup sliced celery
½ cup chopped green pepper
¼ cup chopped, fresh parsley
5 tablespoons flour
¼ teaspoon salt
½ teaspoon garlic salt
3 cups milk
1½ cups grated mild Cheddar cheese
2 pounds cooked shrimp

Melt butter in heavy saucepan. Stir in curry powder, celery, green pepper and parsley; sauté 4 to 5 minutes. Stir in flour all at once and cook, stirring constantly, until flour expands. Gradually add milk, stirring constantly, and stir until mixture thickens and begins to boil. Remove from heat, add salt and garlic salt; blend in cheese. Stir in shrimp and cook over low heat until shrimp is hot. Serve over cooked rice.

Serves 4 to 6

Shrimp and Vegetables

6 ounces uncooked macaroni twirls or green spinach noodles
¼ cup butter
¼ cup flour
3 cups milk
½ teaspoon salt
¼ teaspoon nutmeg
4 ounces grated Cheddar cheese
2 16-ounce packages frozen shrimp, thawed and drained
1 cup sliced carrots
1 cup sliced zucchini
1 cup sliced fresh mushrooms
1 cup chopped broccoli
1 cup snow pea pods, stem and string removed
½ cup chopped onion

Cook macaroni according to package directions, rinse in cold water and drain. Melt butter; stir in flour and cook, stirring constantly, until flour expands and mixture is smooth. Gradually stir in milk and bring to a boil, stirring constantly. Add salt, nutmeg, cheese and shrimp; cook two minutes, stirring constantly. Reduce heat to low. In large bowl, microwave carrots 3 minutes on high; add remaining ingredients and microwave 3 minutes longer. (Vegetables will be partially cooked and quite crisp.) Combine hot sauce, noodles and vegetables. If desired, sprinkle with grated Parmesan cheese before serving.

Serves 6

On July 7, 1959, Milwaukee was host to nobility from Great Britain. The visiting royalty were none less than Her Majesty, Queen Elizabeth II, and Prince Philip; the momentous occasion was the opening of the St. Lawrence Seaway. This event marked the initiation of Wisconsin ports into world-wide commerce.

Crab and Cheese Supreme
"Fit for royalty"

6 to 8 slices buttered toast
2 cups flaked crab
½ pound grated Swiss cheese
3 eggs
1 cup light cream
1 cup milk
¼ teaspoon salt
⅛ teaspoon pepper
Paprika

Line the bottom of a buttered 9 x 13-inch baking pan with toast; layer with crab and cheese. Beat eggs until lemon colored; combine with cream, milk, salt and pepper. Pour over casserole. Sprinkle with paprika. Bake in 325° oven 50 minutes or until set.

Serves 8

Italians have a great respect and love for their cuisine, much of which uses pastas and cheese. Since the industrial cities along Lake Michigan have large Italian communities, the Wisconsin cheese producers found a ready-made market for their Italian cheeses.

Italian Pasta Stuffing

"Cheesey"

1 pound Ricotta cheese
¼ pound Mozzarella cheese
½ cup freshly grated Parmesan cheese
½ cup freshly grated Romano cheese
3 tablespoons finely chopped pecans
2 tablespoons chopped parsley
3 beaten eggs
1 teaspoon salt
⅛ teaspoon freshly ground pepper
⅛ teaspoon freshly grated nutmeg

Break up Ricotta into chunks; combine with remaining ingredients and mix thoroughly. Stuff into any large pastas, cover with your favorite Italian sauce and bake.

Makes about 2½ cups

Green Chilies and Cream Cheese Steak Sauce

1 **tablespoon finely minced canned green chilies**
1 **medium onion, finely minced**
½ **cup olive oil**
4 **cloves garlic, minced**
½ **cup red wine vinegar**
½ **teaspoon salt**
3 **ounces cream cheese**

Combine chilies, onion, garlic, olive oil, vinegar and salt; set aside 3 hours. Add cream cheese and beat well. Spread over broiled or grilled meats.

Makes 1 cup

Barbecue Sauce for Ribs or Chicken

3 **tablespoons olive oil**
⅓ **cup minced onion**
1 **cup catsup**
⅓ **cup vinegar or lemon juice**
3 **tablespoons brown sugar**
½ **cup dark molasses**
½ **cup water**
2 **teaspoons prepared mustard**
⅛ **teaspoon salt**

Sauté onions in olive oil until golden. Add remaining ingredients and simmer, covered, for 15 minutes.

Makes 2 cups

Sweets and Treats

Around 1905 Frank Sloup joined a loggers camp near Oconto. He was about 16 years old and was slight of build so they made him a cooks helper or "cookie." This is a recipe he remembered and passed on to his grandchildren, who are passing it on to us.

Shoepac Pie
"A rich butterscotch pie"

3 tablespoons butter
2 cups firmly packed
   brown sugar
1⅔ cups water, boiling
1 teaspoon vanilla
4 tablespoons cornstarch
2 tablespoons flour
½ teaspoon salt
2 tablespoons sugar
½ cup cold water
4 egg yolks, lightly beaten
1 baked pastry shell for
   9-inch pie
   Meringue

Melt butter in heavy saucepan; add brown sugar. Stir over low heat until well blended. Add boiling water and vanilla; bring to a boil, stirring constantly. Continue to stir and boil until mixture turns a glossy dark brown. Mix together cornstarch, flour, salt and sugar; add cold water and mix until a smooth paste. Slowly add paste, stirring constantly, to boiling syrup. Reduce heat and cook, stirring constantly, until mixture thickens. Gradually stir in egg yolks. Increase heat and cook until thick, stirring constantly. Pour into baked 9-inch pastry shell and let cool. Cover with meringue and sprinkle lightly with powdered sugar. Bake in 450° oven for 5 to 10 minutes, until meringue is golden brown.

Makes 1 pie

Some of the best sailing in the U.S. is around the Apostle Islands of Lake Superior, because they provide natural protection for "smooth sailing." The Islands were designated as National Lakeshore in 1969 because of their miles of beautiful wilderness. Madeline Island is the largest and best known of the Apostle Islands.

Lemon-Cheese Pie
"Smooth sailing"

8 ounces cream cheese
2 tablespoons butter
½ cup sugar
1 egg
2 tablespoons flour
⅔ cup half-and-half
¼ cup fresh lemon juice
2 tablespoons grated lemon peel
1 graham cracker crust for a 9-inch pie

Cream together cream cheese and butter; add sugar and egg and beat well. Stir in flour and cream, mixing well. Blend in lemon juice and lemon peel. Pour into crust, sprinkle with additional crust crumbs if desired and bake in a 350° oven 35 to 40 minutes. Refrigerate before serving.

Makes 1 pie

Crumb Crust

1½ cups finely crushed graham cracker crumbs
⅓ cup sugar
6 tablespoons melted butter
1 teaspoon cinnamon*

Toss together the crumbs and sugar; drizzle butter over top and cut with a fork until crumbs are well-moistened. Mix in cinnamon, if desired. Reserve 3 tablespoons of buttered crumbs for topping; press the remainder into a 9-inch pie pan. Chill thoroughly before filling, or bake in a 350° oven 7 to 10 minutes.

*optional   **Makes 1 pie crust**

Recipes from Wisconsin with Love...

The international headquarters for The Society for the Preservation and Encouragement of Barber Shop Quartet Singing in America is located in Kenosha. The combination of the four fruits in the following pie gives it a very unique, but harmonious, flavor, just as the juxtaposition of four diverse voices in barbershop quartet singing blends into their distinctive sound.

Harmony Pie

½ cup butter
1½ cups sugar
1 teaspoon vanilla
¾ teaspoon salt
1¼ cups flour
¾ cup oatmeal
1½ cups diced fresh rhubarb
1 tablespoon water
3 egg yolks
1½ cups diced pineapple, fresh or canned and drained

1½ cups sliced strawberries, fresh or frozen, thawed and drained
1 banana, sliced
½ teaspoon nutmeg
Meringue:
3 egg whites
⅛ teaspoon salt
⅓ cup sugar
½ teaspoon vanilla or lemon extract flavoring

Makes 1 pie

Cream together butter, ¼ cup of the sugar, vanilla and ½ teaspoon of the salt. Stir in 1 cup of the flour and the oatmeal, blending until a dough is formed. Press dough evenly over bottom and sides of a 10-inch pie pan, shaping a high, even edge. Chill. Mix together remaining sugar, flour and salt; set aside. Combine rhubarb and water in a saucepan; cover and bring to a boil. Stir in the reserved sugar mixture; bring back to a boil, stirring constantly. Beat egg yolks until lighter in color. Pour ½ cup of hot rhubarb mixture into yolks slowly, stirring constantly; gradually add to remaining hot rhubarb mixture, stirring constantly until thick. Remove from heat. Arrange pineapple, strawberries and banana in chilled pie shell; sprinkle with nutmeg. Pour rhubarb mixture over fruits. Bake in a 375° oven 30 minutes or until set.

Make meringue by beating egg whites and salt together until soft peaks form. Gradually add sugar, beating constantly, until stiff peaks form. Fold in flavoring. Spread over baked filling and bake in 375° oven 8 to 10 minutes or until lightly browned.

In the early 1900's this flavorful treat would have been made with heavy cream which had been skimmed into a crock to prepare for baking. Now, commercial sour cream stands in admirably for making this favorite dessert.

Sour Cream Raisin Pie
"Top of the barrel"

1 cup raisins
Water
1 cup sugar
1 cup sour cream
3 egg yolks
1/4 to 1/2 teaspoon cloves
Dash of salt
1 unbaked pastry shell for 9-inch pie

Meringue:
3 egg whites
1/4 cup sugar

In a saucepan, pour enough water over raisins to cover and bring to a boil; boil 1 minute and drain. Combine sour cream, egg yolks, cloves and salt and beat well. Fold in raisins. Pour into the unbaked pastry shell and bake in 325° oven 40 to 45 minutes or until set. Cool slightly. Whip egg whites until soft peaks form. Gradually add sugar, whipping constantly until peaks are stiff. Do not overbeat. Spread over pie and return to oven for 10 to 15 minutes, until meringue is lightly browned.

Makes 1 pie

The violet was chosen as Wisconsin's state flower by a vote of school-children on Arbor Day in 1909. When you are out scouting for the 20 varieties of violets which grow wild in Wisconsin, pick enough black-berries for this scrumptious pie.

Blackberry Cream Pie

1 cup plus 2 tablespoons sugar
1 cup sour cream
3 tablespoons flour
$\frac{1}{8}$ teaspoon salt
4 cups fresh blackberries
1 unbaked pastry shell for a 9-inch pie
$\frac{1}{4}$ cup dry bread crumbs
1 tablespoon butter, melted

Violets

Blackberry

Combine sugar, sour cream, flour and salt; stir well. Arrange blackberries in bottom of pastry shell and sprinkle 1 tablespoon sugar over berries. Spread sour cream mixture on berries. Mix together bread crumbs, remaining table-spoon sugar and melted butter and sprinkle over sour cream mixture. Bake in preheated 375° oven 45 to 50 minutes or until center is firm.

Makes 1 pie

Recipes from Wisconsin with Love...

After a stimulating evening in an open-air theater, it can be most gratifying to sit over coffee and a rich dessert to "digest the drama." The American Players Theater in Spring Green dedicates itself to classical theater and brings in celebrity performers for its high quality productions. On a theater evening, or any evening, this dessert is a perfect climax.

Show-Stopper Pie

"A rich cheese custard"

1 cup sour cream
1 cup grated Swiss cheese
4 eggs
1/3 cup sugar
1 tablespoon vanilla
2 cups milk
1/4 to 1/2 teaspoon nutmeg
1 cup whipping cream
2 tablespoons
   powdered sugar
2 ounces unsweetened
   chocolate, grated
1 unbaked pastry shell for
   9-inch pie

Combine sour cream and cheese in a saucepan and heat, stirring constantly, just until cheese melts. Do not boil. Remove from heat and cool 20 minutes. Add eggs, one at a time, beating well after each addition. Stir in sugar and vanilla. Gradually add milk, beating constantly. Pour into the pastry shell, sprinkle with nutmeg and bake in 350° oven 40 minutes or until a knife inserted in center comes out clean. Cool and refrigerate. Before serving, beat whipping cream until thick, add powdered sugar and beat just until stiff. Fold grated chocolate in by hand and spread over pie.

Makes 1 pie

The Annual Apple Festival held in Bayfield each October just might be the last chance to get out of the cities and enjoy the kaleidoscope of colors of autumn in Wisconsin before the first snow flies.

Apple Crumb Pie
"Everybody's favorite"

4 or 5 large tart apples
1 unbaked pastry shell for 9-inch pie
1 cup sugar
1 teaspoon cinnamon
¾ cup flour
⅓ cup butter

Pare, halve and slice apples; arrange in pastry shell. Mix together ½ cup sugar and cinnamon; sprinkle over apples. Cut butter into remaining ½ cup sugar and flour until mixture resembles coarse meal. Sprinkle on top of pie. Bake in preheated 375° oven 40 to 50 minutes or until apples are bubbly and topping is nicely browned.

Makes 1 pie

Short Crust Pastry

Makes a single crust pastry shell

1 cup flour*
¼ teaspoon salt
¼ cup butter or margarine
3 or 4 tablespoons water

Combine flour and salt. Rub bits of margarine into flour using fingertips, until mixture resembles coarse meal. Add just enough water to hold pastry together. Turn onto a lightly floured surface, knead two or three turns then roll into circle ⅛-inch thick. Fit into a 9-inch pie pan and crimp edges. If crust is to be baked before filling, score edges and bottom with a fork and bake in a 450° oven 10 to 12 minutes or until lightly browned.

*For a double crust pie, increase flour to 1⅔ cup, salt to ½ teaspoon and add ⅓ cup lard or shortening with the same amount of butter as above.

This cheesecake is like the bald eagle. It's better with nothing on top. Wisconsin boasts one of the biggest populations of bald eagles anywhere. In 1982 there were 180 nesting pairs.

Cheesecake
"Doesn't need any help"

16 **ounces cream cheese**
3 **eggs**
2/3 **cup sugar**
1/8 **teaspoon almond**
   flavoring
Topping:
1 **pint sour cream**
1 **teaspoon vanilla**
3 **tablespoons sugar**

Beat cream cheese until softened. Add eggs, one at a time, beating well after each addition. Stir in sugar and almond flavoring and beat for 5 minutes. Pour into a greased and lightly floured 8 or 9-inch round cake pan and bake in preheated 325° oven for 50 minutes. Cool 20 minutes. Stir together topping ingredients and beat well. Pour onto cooled cake, return to oven for 15 more minutes.

Makes 1 round cake

Baked cheesecake offers a great means to enjoy fresh cherries from Door County. If you don't have access to that special treat, a can of dark red pitted tart cherries can do.

Baked Cheese Cake

"Great with fruit topping"

1 18½-ounce package yellow cake mix
4 eggs
2 tablespoons vegetable oil
16 ounces cream cheese
½ cup sugar
1½ cups milk
3 tablespoons lemon juice
1 tablespoon vanilla
1 16-ounce can pie filling

Reserve 1 cup of cake mix. In large bowl combine remainder of cake mix with 1 egg and oil and cut with fork until mixture is crumbly. Press onto bottom and sides of a greased 9 x 13-inch baking pan. Blend together cream cheese, sugar, the 3 remaining eggs and the reserved cake mix. Beat well. Stir in milk, lemon juice and vanilla. Pour into crust and bake in preheated 300° oven 50 to 55 minutes until center is firm. Cool (the top will often crack as the cake cools). Spread the filling of your choice over the top and serve.

Makes a 9x13-inch cake

Wisconsin Apple Cake

4 cups pared, diced apples
2 cups sugar
1 cup coarsely chopped
   pecans or walnuts
1 cup raisins
1 teaspoon grated
   lemon rind
3 cups flour
½ teaspoon cinnamon
½ teaspoon salt
½ teaspoon baking soda
3 eggs
1 cup vegetable oil
1 teaspoon vanilla

Toss together apples, sugar, nuts, raisins and lemon rind; set aside 1 hour to allow juices to form, stirring occasionally. Combine flour, cinnamon, salt and baking soda. Beat eggs; gradually add oil and vanilla, beating constantly. Pour the egg mixture at once into the dry ingredients and stir just until moistened. Batter will be lumpy. Add apple mixture and stir to blend well. Pour batter into a buttered 9-inch round baking pan. Bake in a preheated 350° oven 1½ hours or until a knife inserted in the center comes out clean.

Makes a round layer cake

The wild cranberry has long flourished in the marshy bogs of Wisconsin. However, the progress in the commercial production of cranberries is largely due to the research efforts of the University of Wisconsin. Today, Wisconsin ranks second in the nation for commercially grown cranberries.

Wisconsin Cranberry Cake

1½   cups quartered
       cranberries
1   cup chopped dates
¾   chopped pecans
1   tablespoon vanilla
2½   cups flour
½   cup butter
1¾   cups plus 2 tablespoons
       sugar
2   eggs
2   tablespoons grated
       orange rind
1   teaspoon baking soda
1   teaspoon baking powder
1   cup buttermilk
⅔   cup orange juice

Combine cranberries, dates and nuts; sprinkle with vanilla, toss with ½ cup flour and set aside. Cream together butter and 1¼ cups of the sugar; add eggs, one at a time, beating well after each addition. Stir in orange rind. Combine remaining 2 cups flour, soda and baking powder; add to creamed mixture alternately with buttermilk, beating well after each addition. Fold in reserved cranberry mixture and pour into a buttered tube pan. Bake in a preheated 350° oven 1 hour. Cool 15 minutes. Heat orange juice with remaining ⅔ cup sugar until sugar is dissolved. Invert cake from pan onto wire rack. Pour orange juice mixture over cake, catching drippings and pouring back over cake. Cover and refrigerate at least 10 hours. Note: This cake can be baked up to a week ahead of serving. It's great at holiday time.

Makes 1 tube cake

Banana Spice Cake

1 **cup butter**
1½ **cups sugar**
3 **eggs**
3½ **cups flour**
3 **teaspoons baking powder**
½ **teaspoon baking soda**
1½ **teaspoons cloves**
1½ **teaspoons cinnamon**
¼ **cup honey**
1½ **cups milk**
1½ **cups mashed ripe banana**
1 **cup chopped walnuts**

Cream together butter and sugar; add eggs, one at a time, beating well after each addition. Combine flour, baking powder, baking soda, cloves and cinnamon. Blend together honey, milk and banana. Stir dry ingredients into creamed mixture alternately with banana mixture, beating well after each addition. Pour into a greased and lightly floured 9 x 13-inch baking pan and bake in a 325° oven 1 hour or until cake tests done. Frost with a cream cheese frosting when cooled.

Makes a 9 x 13-inch cake

Recipes from Wisconsin with Love...

Wisconsin is the only state that commercially produces sphagnum moss, a plant that can hold 20 times its weight in water. This makes it most useful in the shipping of plants and in hydroponic gardening. Sphagnum moss grows in the marshy wetlands, and takes three years to mature for harvest.

Moss Cake

'Eggs-elent'

11	egg yolks
1	cup sugar
1/8	teaspoon salt
1	teaspoon cinnamon
1/2	teaspoon cloves
1	teaspoon baking powder
1/4	cup flour
1/2	cup chopped nuts
3	egg whites

Beat together egg yolks, sugar and salt for 15 minutes, until mixture is pale lemon in color and very thick. Combine spices, baking powder, flour and nuts; add to egg yolk mixture and blend well. Beat egg whites just until stiff peaks begin to form and fold carefully into the yolk batter. Pour into an ungreased tube or bundt pan; bake in 325° oven 45 minutes. Increase oven temperature to 350° and bake another 15 minutes.

Makes 1 tube cake

Ehrich Weiss, known to millions as Harry Houdini, was born in Appleton in 1874. A famous magician and escape artist, he practiced as a child by picking the locks on his mother's pastry cupboard and escaping with his choice of the forbidden cakes and cookies.

Magical Poppyseed Cake
"It disappears before your eyes"

¾ **cup poppyseeds**
¾ **cup milk**
¾ **cup butter**
1½ **cups sugar**
2 **cups flour**
3 **teaspoons baking powder**
   Dash of salt
1 **teaspoon vanilla**
4 **egg whites**

Soak poppyseeds in the milk for 2 or more hours. Cream together the butter and sugar. Stir in poppyseeds and milk. Combine flour, baking powder and salt; stir into creamed mixture and beat well. Beat egg whites just until stiff peaks begin to form and fold carefully into the batter. Pour into a greased 9 x 13-inch baking pan and bake in a preheated 350° oven 25 minutes or until cake tests done.

Makes a 9x13-inch cake

Recipes from Wisconsin with Love...

The bad economic conditions around the mines of Cornwall, England, sent droves of Cornishmen to the Wisconsin lead mines between 1830 and 1850. It was estimated that 8500 settled in Lafayette, Iowa and Grant Counties. With them they brought many Old Country recipes, such as pasty, heavy cakes and saffron bread. As lead became harder to find, the miners either joined in the California gold rush or turned to agriculture.

Cornish Heavy Cakes

1 **cup raisins**
2 **cups water**
3 **cups flour**
1 **cup sugar**
1 **teaspoon nutmeg**
1 **teaspoon soda**
1 **teaspoon salt**
1 **teaspoon baking powder**
1 **cup shortening**
½ **cup buttermilk**
1 **teaspoon lemon extract flavoring**

Bring raisins and water to a boil; reduce heat and simmer 5 minutes. Drain and set aside. Combine flour, sugar, nutmeg, baking soda, salt and baking powder, stirring to blend well. Cut in shortening until mixture resembles coarse meal. Add the drained raisins, buttermilk and lemon extract, stirring just to blend. Mixture will be lumpy. Pat dough on a lightly floured surface until ¼-inch thick; cut into 2½ or 3-inch rounds with a cookie or biscuit cutter. Sprinkle with sugar. Bake on ungreased cookie sheets in 350° oven 15 minutes.

Makes 1½ dozen

The sugar maple is Wisconsin's state tree. If you like to get to the source of things, you have a chance to see how maple syrup is made at the Wisconsin Maple Sugar Festival in Aniwa in May. There you can also taste fresh syrup served over pancakes at a rate of 15 plates a minute, which attests to the popularity of this delicacy. There are other ways to enjoy maple syrup and other maple festivals as well. For example, at the Bubolz Nature Preserve's Super Syrup Day, they'll introduce you to the joy of eating it on ice cream. The avid do-it-yourselfer can find workshops which offer instruction in the process of making maple syrup, which can then be used in the following cake recipe.

Maple Syrup Cake

⅓ cup shortening
½ cup sugar
¾ cup maple syrup
2¼ cups cake flour
3 teaspoons baking powder
¼ teaspoon salt
½ cup milk
3 egg whites

Frosting:
3 cups powdered sugar
2 tablespoons cold, strong coffee
1 tablespoon melted butter
⅛ teaspoon maple extract flavoring
3 to 5 tablespoons whipping cream or half-and-half
⅓ cup chopped nuts

Cream together shortening and sugar until fluffy. Stir in syrup. Combine flour, baking powder and salt; add to creamed mixture alternately with milk, beating well after each addition. Beat egg whites until stiff peaks begin to form; fold carefully into the batter. Pour batter into a greased and floured 9 x 9-inch baking pan. Bake in a preheated 350° oven 40 to 45 minutes or until tested done. To make frosting, combine sugar, coffee, butter, flavoring and just enough cream to beat to a spreading consistency. Sprinkle nuts over frosted cake.

Makes a 9 x 9-inch cake

Chocolate Angel Food Cake
"A slice of heaven"

¼ **cup cocoa**
¾ **cup cake flour**
1¾ **cup sugar**
1½ **cups egg whites**
1½ **teaspoons cream of**
  tartar
¼ **teaspoon salt**
1½ **teaspoons vanilla**

Combine cocoa and flour and sift together 3 times. Add 1 cup sugar and sift again 3 times. In large mixing bowl, combine egg whites, cream of tartar, salt and vanilla; beat until foamy. Gradually add the remaining sugar, 2 tablespoons at a time, beating until stiff peaks form. Gradually sift the cocoa mixture over the meringue, a third of a cup at a time, folding carefully after each addition, just until dry ingredients disappear. Spread batter into an ungreased tube pan and carefully cut through the batter with a knife to remove air bubbles. Bake in preheated 375° oven 30 to 35 minutes. Invert and leave in pan until thoroughly cooled.

Makes 1 tube cake

Boiled White Frosting
"Takes practice"

1½ **cups sugar**
⅔ **cup hot water**
    Dash of salt
½ **teaspoon white**
    corn syrup
2 **egg whites**
1 **teaspoon vanilla**

Combine sugar, water, salt and corn syrup. Stir until sugar dissolves. Bring mixture slowly to a boil, stirring constantly. Reduce heat and boil without stirring until candy thermometer reaches 238° to 240° or it makes a string when you lift the spoon. Remove from stove. Beat egg whites until soft peaks form. Beating constantly, pour syrup in a thin stream into the egg whites. Add vanilla and continue beating until frosting holds its shape.

Makes about 2 cups

Mable's Chocolate Frosting

2 **ounces unsweetened**
    chocolate
1 **cup sugar**
⅓ **cup shortening or**
    margarine
½ **teaspoon salt**
1 **teaspoon vanilla**

Combine chocolate, sugar, shortening and salt in a heavy saucepan. Bring slowly to a boil, stirring constantly until sugar dissolves and chocolate melts. Cover and boil 1 minute. Place pan in ice cold water and beat until mixture is of spreading consistency. Stir in vanilla.

Makes 1½ cups

Creamy Rice Pudding

¼ **teaspoon salt**
⅔ **cup sugar**
1 **teaspoon cinnamon***
4 **cups milk**
3 **tablespoons**
   uncooked rice

Combine salt, sugar and cinnamon with 1 cup of milk; blend well. Pour in remainder of the milk and stir in rice. Pour into a buttered 1½ quart casserole and bake in a 300° oven 3½ hours, stirring occasionally during the first hour of baking to prevent rice from sticking on bottom.

*Grated orange or lemon rind can be substituted for the cinnamon. Raisins can be added, if desired.

4 to 6 Servings

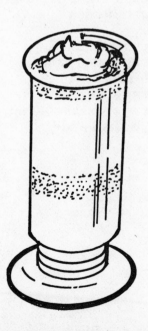

The melodious words of various Indian languages have embellished Wisconsin with a symphony of sounds. The music of these languages, past and present, echoes from the names of the multitudes of lakes, rivers, towns and counties. Even many of the names of the tribes are lyrical: Menomonee, Potawatami, Winnebago, Munsee, Oneida, Stockbridge, Chippewa (Ojibwa), Mascoutin, Ottawa, Sioux, Fox, Sauk, Miami, Illinois and Kickapoo.

Cranberry Pudding
"Rich and yummy"

1 cup sugar
2 cups flour
2 teaspoons baking powder
1 cup milk
3 tablespoons melted butter
2 cups whole or halved cranberries

Sauce:
½ cup butter
1 cup firmly packed brown sugar
¾ cup sugar
¼ cup dark corn syrup
¾ cup half-and-half

Mix together sugar, flour and baking powder. Stir in milk and melted butter until batter is smooth. Add cranberries. Pour into a greased 9 x 9-inch baking pan. Bake in a preheated 350° oven 45 minutes. To make sauce, combine all ingredients in a heavy saucepan. Bring slowly to a boil, stirring constantly. Boil, uncovered, until candy thermometer reaches 228°. Serve warm sauce over individual squares of pudding.

Makes a 9 x 9-inch cake

Orange "Mousse"

6 ounces coarsely
chopped white
chocolate
2 egg yolks
¼ cup powdered sugar
2 tablespoons orange
flavored liqueur
2 cups whipping cream

Melt chocolate, stirring constantly, in top of double boiler set over hot—not boiling—water. In large mixing bowl, beat egg yolks until thick and lemon colored, add sugar and continue beating until light and fluffy. Stir in liqueur and chocolate. Beat whipping cream until stiff. Stir a third of the cream into the yolk mixture, then gently fold in the remainder of the cream, just until blended. Spoon into sherbet or parfait glasses and refrigerate at least 2 hours.

4 to 6 Servings

Chocolate "Mousse"

6 ounces dark sweetened
chocolate, coarsely
chopped
2 egg yolks
¼ cup powdered sugar
2 tablespoons brandy
2 cups whipping cream

Melt chocolate, stirring constantly, in top of double boiler set over hot—not boiling—water. In large mixing bowl, beat egg yolks until thick and lemon colored, add sugar and continue beating until light and fluffy. Stir in brandy and chocolate. Beat whipping cream until stiff. Stir a third of the cream into the yolk mixture, then gently fold in the remainder of the cream just until blended. Spoon into sherbet or parfait glasses and refrigerate at least 2 hours.

4 to 6 servings

Recipes from Wisconsin with Love...

The Wisconsin Dells were formed 15,000 years ago by glacial activity, and more recently by human enterprise. A wide array of tourist attractions combine with the rugged natural beauty to create a popular vacation spot. The Winnebago Indians believed that long ago the Great Spirit, in the body of a snake, forced itself through a narrow opening in the rocks, carving out the Dells. Today, excursion boats follow the path of the snake through the fantastic sandstone formations.

Rhubarb Crunch

2½ **cups flour**
⅔ **cup powdered sugar**
1 **cup butter or margarine**
3 **cups sugar**
1½ **teaspoons baking powder**
Dash of salt
4 **cups sliced rhubarb**
4 **eggs**

Combine 2 cups flour, sugar and butter, cutting until mixture resembles coarse meal. Press into sides and bottom of a 9 x 13-inch baking pan. Bake in 350° oven 12 to 15 minutes or until lightly browned. Combine remaining flour, sugar, baking powder and salt. Beat eggs well; stir in rhubarb. Add the dry ingredients to the rhubarb mixture and stir well. Pour into the baked crust. Bake in 350° oven 35 to 40 minutes.

Makes a 9 x 13-inch dessert

Strawberry Dessert

1½ cups graham cracker
    crust mix
¾ cup butter
2½ cups powdered sugar
3 eggs
2 tablespoons cornstarch
1 tablespoon sugar
1 10-ounce package
    frozen strawberries,
    thawed
    Whipping cream,
    sweetened and whipped

Press graham cracker crumb crust into bottom of a 9 x 9-inch square baking pan. Cream together butter and powdered sugar; add eggs, one at a time, beating well after each addition. Whip until light and creamy; spread over crust. Combine cornstarch and sugar. Drain strawberry juice into the top of a double boiler. Stir in the cornstarch mixture and thicken, stirring constantly, over boiling water. Fold in strawberries, cool and spread over creamed layer. Refrigerate. Serve with a dollop of sweetened, whipped cream.

9 Servings

One of the two largest bicycle races in the U.S., the Grand Prix of Cycling, wheels its way around some of Wisconsin's beautiful rolling countryside each summer. Visitors and local people, contenders and spectators are all whisked into the healthy fervor of this energetic sport. The course runs from Madison to Fond du Lac to Oshkosh to Ripon to Green Lake to Appleton and back to Oshkosh.

Pedaller's Apple and Cheese Squares

"Tastes best chilled"

1½ cups unsweetened applesauce*
⅓ cup honey or pure maple syrup
1 teaspoon cinnamon
1¼ cups grated Cheddar, Edam or Gouda cheese
1½ cup oatmeal
1¼ cup wheat germ
¼ teaspoon salt
¼ cup chopped pecans
1 tablespoon brown sugar

Combine applesauce, honey, cinnamon and 1 cup cheese; stir well. Combine oatmeal, wheat germ and salt; spread half over bottom of a greased 9 x 13-inch baking pan. Cover with applesauce mixture and top with remaining oatmeal mixture. Sprinkle with pecans, brown sugar and remaining cheese. Cover and bake in 350° oven 30 minutes. Uncover and bake an additional 10 minutes.

*if applesauce is sweetened, omit honey.

12 Servings

Wisconsin is respected world wide for its winter sports. The famous "Birkebeiner" cross country skiing competition is the largest in North America, attracting some 6000 applicants for the grueling race from Hayward to Cable. At Timber Coulee, near Westby, ski jumpers compete for national recognition. There are numerous other recreational ski areas to choose from. Other winter sports include ice fishing, ice skating, snowmobiling, hockey, broomball, curling bonspiel, dog sledding, ice sailing and even ice harness races at Lake Geneva. Many of the state's resorts now promote winter tourism for those who want to enjoy the snowy wonderland.

Fudgy Oatmeal Bars
"Calories can't count"

2 cups firmly packed brown sugar
1 cup butter
2 eggs
2 teaspoons vanilla
2½ cups flour
1 teaspoon baking soda
1 teaspoon salt
3 cups old-fashioned or quick-cooking oatmeal
1 12-ounce package semi-sweet chocolate chips
1 14-ounce can sweetened condensed milk
2 tablespoons butter
1 cup chopped nuts

Cream together brown sugar and butter. Add eggs, one at a time, beating well after each addition. Combine flour, baking soda and ½ teaspoon of the salt; stir into creamed mixture, blending well. Add 1 teaspoon vanilla and the oatmeal; stir well. Reserve a third of the oatmeal batter. Press remaining two-thirds batter into a greased 15¼ x 10-inch jelly roll pan. Combine chocolate chips, milk and butter in a heavy saucepan, stirring constantly over medium heat until chips are melted. Remove from heat, stir in nuts, remaining teaspoon of vanilla and ½ teaspoon salt. Spread this mixture over batter. Drop reserved batter by rounded teaspoons onto the chocolate mixture. Bake in a preheated 350° oven 25 to 30 minutes. While warm, cut into bars.

Makes 6 dozen

No Bake Bars
"Good when you're in a jam"

½ **cup sugar**
½ **cup dark corn syrup**
¾ **cup smooth peanut butter**
3 **cups corn flakes**
½ **cup caramel or butterscotch chips**
½ **cup semi-sweet chocolate chips**

Combine sugar and syrup in a heavy saucepan, stirring over low heat until sugar dissolves. Bring slowly to a boil; add peanut butter, stirring until well blended. Remove from heat. Mix in corn flakes, stirring to coat evenly. Press into a buttered 9 x 9-inch baking pan. Melt chips in the top of double boiler set over hot, not boiling, water. Spread over corn flakes mixture; cool before cutting into bars.

Makes 1 dozen

Recipes from Wisconsin with Love...

The first Wisconsin State Fair was held October 1-2, 1851, on the Rock County Fairgrounds in Janesville. Today, Milwaukee hosts the much-expanded State Fair, which brings together some of Wisconsin's finest to be shared, compared, admired and savored.

Best-Ever Brownies
"Prize-winning"

4 eggs
1/2 cup butter or margarine
1 cup sugar
1 teaspoon vanilla
1 12-ounce can chocolate syrup
1 cup plus 1 tablespoon flour
1/2 teaspoon baking powder
1/2 cup coarsely chopped walnuts

Frosting:
1 cup sugar
1/4 cup shortening
1/2 cup milk
1/2 cup semi-sweet chocolate chips

Combine eggs, butter, sugar and vanilla; beat well. Blend in chocolate syrup. Add flour and baking powder; beat well. Fold in nuts. Spread into a greased and lightly floured 15¼ x 10-inch jelly roll pan. Bake in a preheated 350° oven 20 to 25 minutes. To make frosting, bring sugar, shortening and milk slowly to a rolling boil; remove from heat. Add chips, stirring until melted. Beat until consistency to spread.

Makes about 6 dozen

A great recipe for stress release is a bike hike through the Sparta-Elroy National Bike Trail. It will chart your way along 32 miles of old railroad bed, and channel you through three tunnels hewn out of the rock. The towering hills and serene dairy farms of the unglaciated "driftless area" help make this an excursion into tranquility. A few choco-toffee bars in your knapsack will not be incompatible...

Choco-Toffee Treats

"Fun to make and better to eat"

2/3 cup butter or margarine
4 1/2 cups old-fashioned or quick-cooking oatmeal
1 cup firmly packed brown sugar
1/2 cup dark corn syrup
1 teaspoon salt
1 tablespoon vanilla
1 12-ounce package semi-sweet chocolate chips

Melt butter in large saucepan and remove from heat. Stir in remaining ingredients, mixing well. Press into a greased 15 1/4 x 10-inch jelly roll pan. Bake in a preheated 450° oven 10 to 12 minutes (Mixture will be brown and bubbly). Cool, invert from pan and cut into bars.

Makes about 6 dozen

Sweets and Treats

Recipes from Wisconsin with Love...

Baraboo was the birthplace and winter home for the Ringling Brothers Circus. Five of the Ringling brothers banded together in 1882 to form the Ringling Brothers Classic and Comic Concert Company, which grew into "The Greatest Show on Earth." The Circus World Museum now occupies their old winter quarters, and with conscientious attention to historic detail, recreates and preserves the circus with all of its flamboyant magic, flash and dazzle.

The Greatest Ginger Snaps on Earth

1 cup sugar
¾ cup margarine
¼ cup dark molasses
1 egg
2 cups flour
2 teaspoons baking soda
1 teaspoon ginger
½ teaspoon cloves
½ teaspoon cinnamon
⅛ teaspoon salt
Sugar

Cream together sugar and margarine. Add molasses and egg; beat well. Combine flour, soda, ginger, cloves, cinnamon and salt. Stir into creamed mixture and beat well. Shape dough into walnut-sized balls and roll in sugar. Place balls onto greased cookie sheets 1½ to 2 inches apart. Bake in preheated 350° oven about 12 minutes. Let cookies cool on baking sheets a few minutes before removing.

Makes 5 dozen

Scandinavian Christmas tradition dictates that to keep the spirit of Christmas from leaving the house, everyone who enters must have a cookie or sweet to eat. Settlers from Scandinavia brought this hospitable practice with them to Wisconsin, where it flourishes year around, ensuring that the Christmas spell of good cheer will not be broken.

Berlina Kranser
"Norwegian cookie"

4 boiled or poached egg yolks
1 cup sugar
2 cups butter
4 raw egg yolks
5 cups flour
Egg white
Sugar

Push cooked egg yolks through a sieve or ricer; mix with sugar until completely combined. Cream the sugar and egg yolk mixture with butter; add raw egg yolks and beat well. Gradually add flour, beating well. Chill at least 1 hour, until dough can be rolled out. To shape each cookie, roll a small ball of dough with the palm of your hand into a pencil-sized stick that is ¼ inch around by 4 or 5 inches long. Cross one end over the other, making a script "ℓ". Beat egg white until frothy; dip each cookie into egg white, sprinkle with sugar and place on greased cookie sheet. Bake in preheated 350° oven 10 to 12 minutes or until golden brown.

Makes 5 dozen

Along with the traditions of Christmas came a repertoire of recipes for sweet delicacies. Krumkake and Berlina Kranser are among the favorites which found their way to Wisconsin. Stoughton claims to be the coffee capital of the world, so these cookies are served there often as a light, crispy companion to that bottomless cup.

Krumkake

"Delicate"

1 cup sugar
3 eggs
1 cup whipping cream or half-and-half
½ cup melted butter
½ teaspoon salt
1 tablespoon vanilla
1¼ cups flour

Beat together sugar and eggs. Stir in cream, butter, salt and vanilla; mix well. Add flour, stirring until well blended. Drop by tablespoon onto a heated krumkake iron and bake until light brown. Remove and immediately roll on a wooden cone to shape.

Makes about 4 dozen

Russian Tea Cakes
"A holiday treat"

1 cup butter
½ cup powdered sugar
½ teaspoon salt
2 teaspoons vanilla
2 cups flour
¾ to 1 cup finely chopped walnuts or pecans
Powdered sugar

Cream together butter and sugar. Add salt, vanilla, flour and nuts; blend well. Chill at least 2 hours. When ready to bake, shape dough into walnut-sized balls and place on ungreased cookie sheets 1½ inches apart. Bake in preheated 350° oven 12 minutes or until lightly browned. While cookies are still warm, roll in powdered sugar. If desired, roll in powdered sugar again after completely cooled.

Makes 5 dozen

The St. Croix River has always been a dynamic force in the development of western Wisconsin. Bill Nye, known mainly for his humorous writings and biting commentaries during the late 1800's, grew up in Hudson on the St. Croix. He described the significance of this river in earlier times: "It was at Hudson that we used to bet on the date when navigation would open in the spring. There were no railroads then. When the first boat whistled in the spring, people left their businesses ...in order to run down to the landing and see the first boat come in." Today, the St. Croix, designated as a wild and scenic river by the U.S. Congress, is still prominent as a beautiful and exciting recreational area, suited especially well to canoeing and camping, and so are the following cookies.

Chocolate Chip Oatmeal Cookies
"Make 'em & take 'em to the river"

1 cup shortening
¾ cup sugar
¾ cup firmly packed brown sugar
2 eggs
1 teaspoon hot water
1 teaspoon vanilla
1½ cups flour
1 teaspoon baking soda
1 teaspoon salt
½ cup chopped walnuts
1 6-ounce package chocolate chips
2 cups oatmeal

Cream together shortening and sugars until fluffy. Beat eggs and add water and vanilla; pour into creamed mixture and beat well. Combine flour, baking soda and salt; stir into creamed mixture and beat well. Stir in nuts, chocolate chips and oatmeal. Shape into walnut-sized balls and bake on greased cookie sheets in a preheated 350° oven 10 to 12 minutes.

Makes 6 dozen

Ojibwa legend has it that the god, Nanabohzo, determined to capture the Great Beaver of Lake Superior, built a dam from the south lakeshore and then proceeded to hurl god-sized fistfuls of dirt into the water in an effort to corral his prey. Each fistful formed one of the Apostle Islands, with a double-fisted pitch creating the largest, Madeline Island. The dam became Long Island, a natural breakwater making this one of the best harbors on the Great Lakes. The bay is called Chequamegon, which is the French version of the Indian word meaning "place of the soft beaver dam." To our knowledge, the Great Beaver still resides in Wisconsin's Great Lake.

Apostle Island Cookies
"Brown sugar delights"

¼ cup light corn syrup
½ cup firmly packed brown sugar
¼ cup butter
½ cup flour
½ teaspoon vanilla
½ cup chopped pecans

Combine corn syrup, brown sugar and butter in heavy saucepan; bring slowly to a boil over medium heat, stirring constantly. Remove from heat. Add flour and vanilla, mixing well. Stir in pecans. Drop batter by teaspoonsful onto foil-lined cookie sheets. Bake in preheated 325° oven 8 to 10 minutes or until browned. Cool and stack in an air-tight container.

Makes about 2 dozen

A drive along Highway 151 in southwest Wisconsin offers a view of the astonishing Dickeyville Grotto. The centerpiece is a marble grotto with the Virgin Mary holding Baby Jesus. Surrounding this are structures and statues made of broken glass, china, pebbles and other bright objects set in cement. This amazing "sermon in stone" was built between 1920 and 1930 by Father Wernerus and his cousin, Mary Wernerus. It was included in "Naives and Visionaries," an exhibit which toured art galleries and museums across the U.S.

Divinity
"White heaven"

4 cups sugar
1 cup light corn syrup
¾ cup water
3 egg whites
1 teaspoon vanilla
1½ cups coarsely chopped walnuts

Combine sugar, corn syrup and water in a heavy saucepan and bring to a boil. Cover 3 minutes, remove lid and boil until candy thermometer reaches 255° or a 6-inch string can be formed. While mixture is boiling, beat the egg whites until stiff peaks form. When syrup has reached the proper temperature, pour slowly in a thin stream over the egg whites, beating constantly. Continue to beat until candy can be dropped onto a buttered surface in dollops and hold its shape. Quickly stir in vanilla and nuts just before dropping. Store in an air-tight container after candy has set.

Makes about 2 pounds

Shot Tower is an unusual mine shaft, dug by hand through a cliff overhanging the Wisconsin River straight down to a cave below. The process which gave Shot Tower its name was this: hot lead was poured through a screen at the top to form the shot. These round balls cooled as they fell through the shaft, landing in a pool of water at the bottom. This ingenious method could produce 5,000-10,000 pounds of lead shot in a day. Shot Tower is now in Tower Hill State Park.

Shot Tower Specialty
"Lighter than lead"

1 cup powdered sugar
1 cup smooth peanut butter
1 cup finely chopped dates
1 cup finely chopped walnuts or pecans
1 1-ounce square semi-sweet chocolate
1 cup semi-sweet chocolate chips
1 1-inch cube paraffin

Mix together sugar, peanut butter, dates and nuts. Shape into walnut-sized balls and refrigerate several hours until firm. In a double boiler, melt together the chocolates and paraffin over hot, not boiling, water. Using teaspoons, dip each ball into the warm chocolate mixture and place on waxed paper until hardened. Store in the refrigerator.

Makes 3 dozen

Peanut Butter Balls

2 cups crunchy-style peanut butter
¾ cup margarine
3 cups Rice Crispies™
1 pound powdered sugar
1 12-ounce package chocolate chips
1 large plain chocolate candy bar
Paraffin

Combine peanut butter, margarine, Rice Crispies™ and powdered sugar. Mix well. Shape into walnut-sized balls. Melt chocolates with one-inch cube of paraffin in top of a double boiler set over hot—not boiling—water. Blend well. Dip each ball in chocolate to coat and remove to waxed paper until chocolate hardens.

Makes 6 dozen

Recipes from Wisconsin with Love...

Two covered bridges remain in Wisconsin as quaint reminders of the olden days. One, located near Cedarburg, was built in the late 1800's and is now a historic site. The other, outside Waupaca, is a faithful reproduction built in 1970. Bridges were probably covered to protect the wooden structures from the weather and to prevent domestic animals from being frightened by the open water as they crossed over. Antiquated by modern transportation systems, these charming "kissing bridges" are nostalgic remnants of the past. This Old Fashioned Fudge might also bring back some timeless memories.

Old Fashioned Fudge
"Chocolate nostalgia"

- 2 cups sugar
- ⅔ cup milk
- 2 ounces unsweetened chocolate
- 2 tablespoons light corn syrup
- ¼ teaspoon salt
- 2 tablespoons butter
- 1 teaspoon vanilla
- ½ cup broken walnuts

Combine sugar, milk, chocolate, corn syrup and salt; stir over medium heat until chocolate melts and sugar dissolves. Bring to a boil, cover 3 minutes, remove the lid and cook without stirring until candy thermometer reaches 234° or until it forms a soft ball when a little is dropped in cold water. Remove from heat carefully and cool, without stirring, until candy reaches 110° on the thermometer. Add butter and vanilla then beat constantly just until mixture begins to lose its sheen. Quickly add the nuts and pour into a buttered pan. When set but not completely cool, cut into squares.

Makes about 1¼ pounds

Cranberry Ice
"Light and colorful"

1½ **cups sugar**
2 **cups water**
4 **cups whole cranberries**
¼ **cup orange juice**

Bring sugar and 1 cup of water to boil and boil 5 minutes. Set aside. Simmer cranberries in the remaining cup of water just until they begin to pop and are soft; cool slightly and push through a sieve. Add the sugar syrup and orange juice to the sieved cranberries and blend well. Pour into a freezer tray or loaf pan and freeze just until edges are solid one inch from the tray. Pour into a mixing bowl and beat with an electric mixer on high speed for several minutes. Return to freezer tray or pan and freeze until solid. Cut into squares to serve.

4 Servings

Cranberry Festivals are held in many communities, including Warrens, Minong, Spooner and Wisconsin Rapids. The festivities are planned to coincide with the harvesting and processing of the brightly-colored berries, a perfect time to start eating the fruits of their labors. Any Cranberry Festival crew would approve of this creative treatment of their versatile product.

Sinful Cranberry Topping
"So good it's sinful"

½ cup butter or margarine
1 cup firmly packed
 brown sugar
1 12-ounce package
 (about 5 cups) whole
 fresh cranberries
½ cup orange liqueur
½ cup whipping cream

Combine butter, sugar, cranberries and liqueur in a heavy saucepan and bring slowly to a boil over medium heat, stirring constantly. Reduce heat, cover and simmer just until berries pop. Remove from heat and stir in cream. Serve warm or at room temperature over plain pound cakes, angel food cakes, fresh fruits or ice cream. Store in the refrigerator.

Makes 4 cups

The very first ice cream sundae was concocted in Two Rivers in 1881. Originally, the chocolate topping on ice cream cost a nickel and was sold only on Sundays. But one weekday, a headstrong young girl wanted one of these treats, saying they could pretend it was Sunday. Her obstinacy changed the fate of the ice cream sundae, for the idea caught on and now we have the option of indulging in a sundae any day of the week.

Chocolate Sauce
"Popular every day"

- 1 **cup sugar**
- ⅔ **cup milk**
- 2 **1-ounce squares unsweetened chocolate**
- 2 **tablespoons light corn syrup**
- ¼ **teaspoon salt**
- 2 **tablespoons butter**
- 1 **teaspoon vanilla**

Combine sugar, milk, chocolate, corn syrup and salt in a heavy saucepan; stir constantly over medium heat just until chocolate melts and sugar dissolves. Remove from heat. Cool slightly, then add butter and vanilla. Serve hot over ice cream. Store in the refrigerator.

Makes about 1¼ cups

Munches and Punches

Superior has the largest group of ore docks concentrated in one area in the world. Minnesota folk call it "The Necklace" because the lights sparkle like strands of a diamond necklace when viewed at night from the hills of its twin port, Duluth, across the bay of Lake Superior.

Lake Superior Whitefish Livers

1½ **pounds whitefish livers**
    Boiling water
½ **cup flour**
½ **teaspoon salt**
¼ **teaspoon paprika**
¼ **teaspoon pepper**
¼ **vegetable oil**
¼ **cup butter**

Pour boiling water over livers and let sit just until livers are lighter in color. Drain and rinse in cold water. Combine flour, salt, paprika and pepper in a small paper bag. Add a few livers and shake to coat well; repeat with remaining livers. Stir oil and butter together over medium high heat until butter is melted and mixture is well blended. Place coated livers in hot oil and fry, 3 to 5 minutes, turning once to brown.

Serves 6 to 8

Whitefish Liver Snacks
"A real delicacy"

Pour boiling water over desired amount of whitefish livers and let sit until livers become lighter in color. Drain. Wrap each liver in a small bacon strip and spear together with a toothpick. Grill over hot charcoals or broil until done. Serve hot.

Makes any amount

Oyster Cracker Snacks
"Kids love 'em"

10 **cups oyster crackers**
 1 **tablespoon dill weed**
 1 **1.18-ounce package Hidden Valley™ herb dressing mix**
½ **teaspoon garlic salt**
¾ **cup vegetable oil**

Combine crackers, dill, dressing mix and garlic salt in a paper bag; shake. Drizzle oil over crackers and shake again. Eat as a snack or as croutons for salads or soups.

Makes 10 cups

Fried Walnuts

 6 **cups water**
 4 **cups walnut halves**
½ **cup sugar**
 Vegetable oil
½ **teaspoon salt**

Pour water into a saucepan; bring to a boil. Add walnuts, allow to return to a boil and cook 1 minute. Drain. Rinse walnuts under hot water; drain again. Combine walnuts and sugar in a large mixing bowl, tossing to mix well. (Heat from the walnuts will dissolve the sugar.) Heat an inch of oil to 350°. Fry walnuts 5 minutes or until golden brown. Drain on paper towels. Sprinkle lightly with the salt. Cool. Store in an airtight container.

Makes 4 cups

Recipes from Wisconsin with Love...

The Braves came to Milwaukee in 1953, won the National League pennant in 1957 and beat the New York Yankees in the World Series. But when their departure left Wisconsin without a Big League baseball team, the situation was rectified with the purchase of the Pilots from Seattle in 1970. This team, swept into the spirit of its new home, was transformed into none other than the Milwaukee Brewers, playing its first game in April, 1970. In 1982 they won the American League Championship and although they lost the World Series to the St. Louis Cardinals, they did not lose the backing of their loyal fans who, under the banner "Brew Crew," turned out in the thousands with a tickertape parade to welcome the Brewers home from this exciting "Suds Series."

Microwave Caramel Popcorn

1   **cup firmly packed brown sugar**
½   **cup margarine or butter**
¼   **cup light corn syrup**
½   **teaspoon salt**
½   **teaspoon baking soda**
4   **quarts popped popcorn**

Makes 4 quarts

Combine sugar, butter, syrup and salt in a bowl. Microwave on high until mixture begins to boil; microwave 2 minutes longer. Stir in soda. Put popcorn in a large paper sack and pour syrup evenly over popcorn. Shake the bag vigorously and place in the microwave oven. Microwave 30 seconds on high. Remove the bag, shake again and microwave 1 minute on high; repeat this step one more time. Pour popcorn onto buttered baking sheets to cool.

Recipes from Wisconsin with Love...

"In heaven there is no beer; That's why we drink it here!" Beer-drinking goes with polka-dancing, which partly explains why more beer is drunk in Wisconsin than in any other state in the union. The balance of the explanation lies in the fact that so much good beer is brewed in Wisconsin. The first brewery opened in 1840 on the lakefront in Milwaukee, which is known as "The Beer Capitol of the World." Since then, over 300 breweries have opened and closed in Wisconsin. Today, there are three major breweries: Miller in Milwaukee (2nd in the nation), Heileman in LaCrosse (4th in the nation), and Pabst in Milwaukee (5th in the nation). There are also four small breweries in operation, which distribute only regionally. They are: Huber in Monroe, Leinenkugel in Chippewa Falls, Steven's Point in Steven's Point and Walter in Eau Claire. Any of these will work equally well in the following recipe.

Wisconsin Beer-Cheese Fondue

"Fun for friends"

¼ cup butter or margarine
¼ cup flour
½ teaspoon salt
¼ teaspoon dry mustard
¾ cup beer
¾ cup milk
¾ teaspoon worchestershire sauce
1 drop hot pepper sauce
1¾ cups grated Cheddar cheese

Melt butter in a fondue pot; blend in flour, salt and mustard. Remove from heat and slowly stir in beer, blending until mixture is smooth. Add milk, worchestershire and hot pepper sauces. Return to heat and stir until mixture thickens and bubbles. Add cheese by handfuls, stirring constantly, until all the cheese is melted. This fondue is good with French or pumpernickel bread cubes or fresh vegetables.

Makes about 4 cups

"Little Miss Muffet sat on a tuffet
Eating her curds and whey.
Along came a spider and sat down beside her,
And said, 'Have you tried curds deep-fried?'"

If Little Miss Muffet sat still long enough to heed this smart little spider, she may have discovered these yummy, hot morsels.

Beer Batter

1 cup commercial
   pancake mix
1 cup stale beer
1 egg, beaten
   Dash of salt
   Cheese curds

Combine all ingredients and blend well. Coat cheese curds or cubes and fry in 350° vegetable oil until golden brown.

Makes about 1½ cups batter

Tee-Totaler's Recipe

1 cup flour
1 tablespoon baking
   powder
½ teaspoon salt
¾ cup milk
¼ to ½ cup water
   Cheese curds (or cubes)

Mix together flour, baking powder, salt and milk, stirring well. Add enough water to make batter just thick enough to stay on the cheese curd. Coat curds and drop in 350° vegetable oil. Fry until golden brown.

Makes about 2 cups batter

Sluff-off Beer Batter

Makes any amount

Pour some Aunt Jemima's Complete Pancake Batter™ mix into a bowl. Add enough stale beer to make a thin batter. Stir in salt and hot pepper sauce to taste and—ZAP—you have instant beer batter.

A Guide to Tasteful Combinations of Cheese and Wine

To take the best advantage of a good wine and a good cheese, the combination should be carefully selected. One can too easily overpower the other. A mild cheese wants a delicate wine; a strong-flavored cheese wants a robust wine. Here are some suggestions for pleasing matches.

Cheese	Wine
Blue	Port, Chianti, Bordeaux, Red Burgundies
Brick, American	Serve with any wine
Camembert	Red Burgundies, Rhine wine
Cheddar and Colby	Red Bordeaux or Burgundy
Gouda	Beaujolais, Chablis
Hickory Smoked	Red Burgundies or Bordeaux
Limburger	Baco Noir Burgundy, Chelois
Monterey Jack	Serve with any wine
Muenster	Red or White Bordeaux
Provolone	Baco Noir Burgundy, Chelois
Swiss	Red Burgundy, Chelois

Apples Grown in Wisconsin with National Recognition

Jonathan	Moderately tart, tender apple. Excellent for eating
McIntosh	Tender, juicy and aromatic. Excellent for eating.
Golden Delicious	Firm, fine-grained. Delicate flavor. Sweet eating apple. Flesh doesn't turn brown when cut. Best all-purpose apple.
Cortland	Delicately textured. Mainly an eating apple.
Rome Beauty	Firm and juicy. Excellent for baking and cooking, which brings out the flavor.
Winesap	Slightly tart, crisp and juicy. Wine-like flavor makes it good eating. Stores well. Also good for cooking and baking. All-around apple.

Cheese and Fruit Combinations

Suitable for appetizer or dessert, cheese and fruit can also form a perfect partnership. Paired properly, they present an elegant array of taste, color and texture. We recommend the following combos.

Cheese	Fruit
Blue and Roquefort	Anjou or Bosc pears, apples
Brick, American	Tokay grapes
Camembert and Brie	Apples, pears, plums (tart)
Cheddar and Colby	Apples (tart), melons
Gouda and Edam	Golden Delicious apples, pineapple, oranges
Muenster	Apples, oranges, seedless grapes
Provolone	Bartlett pears
Swiss	Greening apples, oranges, green grapes

Proper Uses for Apples

Use	Reason	Apple
Applesauce	Rich tart taste, juicy pulp	McIntosh, Wealthy, Lodi, Gravenstein, Baldwin, Yellow Transparent
Baking or open-faced tarts	Retain shape	Cortland, Rome Beauty, Golden Delicious
Appetizers, salads, fruit bowls, eating	Attractive appearance, good texture, flavorful	Red Delicious, McIntosh, Winesap, Jonathan, Cortland, Golden Delicious
Pies	Tart, firm, juicy	Cortland, McIntosh, Yellow Transparent, Golden Delicious, Jonathan, Lodi

1 pound of apples = 3 medium apples = 3 cups sliced apples

Deep-Fried Fruits and Vegetables

½ cup milk
½ cup half-and-half
Dash of nutmeg
Dash of cinnamon
⅔ cup flour
⅓ cup cornstarch
1 teaspoon sugar
1 egg yolk
Fruits and vegetables,
cut in bite-sized pieces

Combine milk, half-and-half, seasonings, flour, cornstarch, sugar and egg yolk; beat well. Pat fruit and vegetables dry with paper toweling and coat in batter. Deep fry in oil heated to 375° until golden brown. Serve fruits with Poppyseed Dressing (page 63); vegetables with Zippy Dip (page 194), Curry Dip (page 193), Beefy Cheese Dip (page 195) or Garlic-Ginger Dip (page 193).

Recipes from Wisconsin with Love...

In the heyday of ore mining the frontier towns in the northwest range areas had a reputation for bawdiness and crime. Visitors to the area were warned: "of Cumberland, Hurley, Hayward and Hell—the first three are tougher than the fourth!" Reminiscent of these spirited towns, the following veggie dips will add lustiness to your roughage.

Curry Dip

¾ **cup mayonnaise**
¾ **cup sour cream**
½ **to 1 teaspoon curry powder**
1 **teaspoon salt**
½ **teaspoon dry mustard**
¼ **teaspoon turmeric**

Combine all ingredients and mix well. Cover and refrigerate until ready to serve. Note: Curries vary in intensity—start with ½ teaspoon curry and add to desired taste.

Makes 1½ cups

Garlic-Ginger Veggie Dip

1 **cup mayonnaise or salad dressing**
1 **cup sour cream**
2 **or 3 cloves garlic, crushed or minced**
2 **or 3 teaspoons ground ginger**
Dash of salt
⅛ **to ¼ teaspoon sugar**

Blend together all ingredients. Refrigerate.

Makes 2 cups

Recipes from Wisconsin with Love...

Fox Lake is the hometown of Bernard "Bunny" Berigan, the famed jazz trumpeter. Popular during the Big Band Era of the 1930's, he was often a featured soloist with other big names like Benny Goodman, Bing Crosby, the Dorsey Brothers and Paul Whiteman. He also led his own orchestra, and his theme song was "I Can't Get Started With You." We know the following dip will help get your social gathering started.

Zippy Dip
"Real Jazzy"

¼ **cup water**
¼ **cup milk**
8 **ounces Ricotta or cottage cheese**
¼ **cup crumbled blue cheese**
1 **cup grated Hot Pepper Jack cheese**
1 **clove garlic, minced**
Dash onion powder
Freshly ground pepper

Combine all the ingredients in a blender and whip until smooth. Chill and serve. This may be used as a salad dressing by adding more milk.

Makes 2½ cups

Beefy Cheese Dip

1 8-ounce package cream
  cheese
1 2½-ounce jar dried beef,
  diced
¼ to ⅓ cup minced
  ripe olives
1 tablespoon minced
  onion
2 tablespoons sour cream
1 tablespoon mayonnaise

Blend together all ingredients. Refrigerate.

Makes about 1½ cups

Shrimp Dip

8 ounces cream cheese
1 4-ounce can broken
  shrimp
½ cup chili sauce
1 tablespoon dried
  minced onion

Combine all ingredients and mix well. Refrigerate before serving.

Makes 1½ cups

Taco Dip

1 cup sour cream
4 ounces cream cheese
  Commercial taco
  seasoning mix
½ head lettuce, shredded
2 large tomatoes, diced
1 cup shredded Cheddar
  cheese
1 green pepper, diced

Combine sour cream and cream cheese; sprinkle in taco seasoning to taste. Spread on the bottom of a plate or shallow casserole. Layer over the sour cream mixture the lettuce, tomatoes, cheese and green pepper. Serve with taco chips.

Makes 4 to 5 cups

Warm Cheese Herb Spread

24 ounces cream cheese
¼ cup milk
¼ cup lemon juice
½ teaspoon marjoram
½ teaspoon oregano
½ teaspoon basil
½ teaspoon thyme
¼ teaspoon garlic
1½ cups cooked, chopped baby shrimp

Beat cream cheese until smooth, gradually add milk and lemon juice, beating constantly. Stir in remaining ingredients. Pour into a 9-inch quiche or pie pan, cover and bake in 350° oven 15 to 20 minutes or until hot. Garnish as desired and serve warm with crackers or vegetables.

Makes about 4 cups

SapSago Cocktail Spread
"A cheese flavored with clover"

½ cup butter
½ cup finely grated SapSago cheese

Whip butter until light; blend in cheese to make a smooth, pale-green spread. Mold onto a serving plate and chill 2 hours. In addition to using as a spread, this can be used as a sandwich butter.

Makes 1 cup

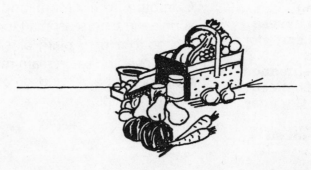

Uncooked Cranberry-Orange Relish

1 pound (4 cups) fresh
   cranberries,
   unblemished and firm
2 large thin-skinned
   oranges, preferably
   seedless
1½ cup sugar

Wash cranberries in cold water and pat dry. Cut oranges into quarters, taking seeds out, leaving skin on. Put cranberries and oranges through coarsest blade of food grinder into a deep bowl. Add sugar, starting with 1 cup and mixing well. Add more sugar to suit taste. Cover bowl with plastic wrap and let stand at room temperature for 24 hours. Can be refrigerated up to 2 or 3 weeks if tightly covered.

Makes 1 quart

Old Military Road, or Ridge Road, was the first to cross the state. Built in the 1830s, it spanned from Green Bay to Prairie du Chien, and opened Wisconsin to all. In 1855, Herbert Quick described his travels over this road: "Here we went, oxen, cows, mules, horses; coaches, carriages, bluejeans, corduroys, rags, tatters, silks, satin, caps, tall hats, poverty, riches; speculators, missionaries, land-hunters, merchants...a nation on wheels, an empire in the commotion and pangs of birth." The most famous stretch of this road was the 25 miles from Pokerville to Dodgeville, which contained at least a dozen saloons. It was along here that the notorious Ridgeway ghost ranged. He was seen by many, both soused and sober, and plagued travelers with mischievous and harmful pranks. His infamy became such that most of life's misfortunes were traced to the Ghost of Ridgeway.

Ready-To-Eat Pickles

"No muss — no fuss"

7 cups sliced cucumbers
1 cup sliced green peppers
1 cup sliced onions
2 tablespoons salt
1 tablespoon celery seed
1 tablespoon dried dill
2 cups sugar
2 cups cider vinegar

Combine cucumbers, green peppers and onions in a large bowl. Sprinkle with seasonings and toss. Pack in pint canning jars. Combine the sugar and vinegar; pour over the pickles to ¾-inch from jar tops. Cover and refrigerate. Pickles will keep 2 or more months in the refrigerator.

Makes 3 pints

Cranberry Rum Slush

12 ounces frozen cranberry
   juice concentrate
12 ounces frozen lemonade
   concentrate
1½ cups water
¾ cup light or dark rum

Blend all ingredients together. Pour into a freezer container and freeze. Mixture will be slushy. To serve, spoon slush into wine glasses.

Serves 6 to 8

Cranberry Vodka Slush

1 3-ounce package cherry,
   strawberry or raspberry
   gelatin
1 cup boiling water
3 cups cold water
12 ounces frozen orange
   juice concentrate
12 ounces frozen lemonade
   concentrate
2 cups vodka
2 cups cranberry juice
   Club soda or 7-up™

Dissolve gelatin in boiling water. Add cold water, orange juice concentrate, lemonade concentrate, vodka and cranberry juice, stirring to blend well. Pour into a large freezer container and freeze. Mixture will be slushy. To serve, mix ¼ to ⅓ cup of slush with club soda or 7-up™ in an ice-filled tumbler.

15 servings

Cranberry Brandy Slush

2 quarts cranberry juice
12 ounces lemonade
   concentrate
1 pint brandy
   7-up™ or gingerale

Mix cranberry juice, lemonade concentrate and brandy together. Pour into a large freezer container and freeze, stirring occasionally. Mixture will be slushy. To serve, mix ¼ to ⅓ cup of slush with 7-up™ or gingerale in an ice-filled tumbler.

20 Servings

Timm's Hill at Ogema is the highest point in Wisconsin, with an elevation of 1951.5 feet. It was dedicated as a county park in the spring of 1983 and a lookout tower was erected on top of the hill next to the old fire tower, which is still operational. Looking from the tower, you can see the fields and fields of Christmas trees for which Ogema is known. The town pays tribute each year on the last weekend in September with the Christmas Tree Festival.

Holiday Tree Decorations

Lots
of
fresh
cranberries
Lots
of
2 to 3-
day-old
unbuttered
popcorn

Make a garland by stringing, in any pattern desired, the cranberries and popcorn, using heavy-duty red thread. Cranberries should be strung through the stem end directly through the center of the fruit; popcorn should be strung through the kernel. After the holidays, drape garland in a tree or on a fence to feed the birds.

Makes any amount

Recipe Index

Subject Index

Contributors

Our thanks to the following great Wisconsin cooks who have shared their favorite recipes with us.

Anderson, Carole	Brookfield	Ladd, Rae	Stoughton
Bednarek, Brygie	Green Lake County	Larson,	Winter
Bednarek, David	Wauwatosa	Lass, Adele	Warrens
Bednarek, Jane	Wauwatosa	Laufenberg, Eleonora	Tomah
Belknap, Carol	Eau Claire	Loescher, Kathy	Beloit
Bengert, Mrs. Paul	Wisconsin Rapids	Lomen, Sandy	Westby
Benkendorf, E.M.	Wauwatosa	Luchini, Barb	Watertown
Beyl, Jean	Madison	Mains, Cheryl	Merrill
Benson, Anne	Westby	Marcott, Wendy	Wilson
Bliss, Donna	Milwaukee	McDonald, Laura	Glidden
Bodin, Beta	Bayfield	Marcott, Dale	Wilson
Bogart, Dick	Delavan	McGrew, Marline	Cedarburg
Bogart, Marcie	Delavan	Michaelson, Gertrude	Ladysmith
Bogart, R.B.	Delavan	Miller, Joe	Beloit
Brandt, Mary	Gays Mills	Miller, Tim	Sun Prairie
Buhrdorf, Ruth	Stonelake	Murray, J. Stephen	Arena
Burnstad, Julie	Tomah	Nereim, Bonnie	Franklin
Burnstad, Rita	Tomah	Nevicosi, Mary	Whitewater
Butz, Sharon	Mauston	Payleitner, Julie	Milwaukee
Calacibetta, Katy	Delavan	Perlich, Caterina	Kenosha
Calkins, Jack	Eau Claire	Pitel, Ann	Tomah
Calkins, Janet	Eau Claire	Roethe, Dick	Sun Prairie
Carley-Hake, Adele	Egg Harbor	Runions, Joan	Alma
Carlton, Patricia	Westby	Schlobohm, Jody	Mayville
Caulkins, Beth	Richland Center	Schroeder, Mabel	Merrill
Chidester, Gail	Delavan	Schroeder, "Orange"	Madison
Cravens, Debra	Madison	Schwab, Lynn	Rice Lake
DeGraff, Peg	Madison	Sherman, Mrs. Stan	Shullsburg
Farley, Mary	Milwaukee	Smatlak, Elizabeth	Rice Lake
Fix, Sue	Brookfield	Smith, Bernard	La Farge
Fortney, S.	Stoughton	Smith, Don	Waupaca
Gerlock, Marlene	Rice Lake	Stewart, Paula	Brookfield
Gluesing, Jeemer	LaCrosse	Stocker, Ann	Shullsburg
Grant, Jan	Antigo	Stocker, Elizabeth	Shullsburg
Grasse, Eileen	Wauwatosa	Stocker, Sue	Shullsburg
Hall, Lena	Glidden	Topitzes, Virginia	Milwaukee
Hansen, Gloria	Egg Harbor	Travanti, Adalgisa	Kenosha
Hass, Paul	Madison	Treutelaar, Mary	Waukesha
Hichlin, Peggy	Baraboo	Tuxford, Edith	Richland Center
Howe, Marion	Siren	Wetli, Viola	Green Bay
Hughes, Donna	Lancaster	Whereatt, Ruthann	Tomah
Hughes, Pearl	Lancaster	Whiting, Ingrid	Delavan
Jensen, Pearl	Wausau	Wichman, Alex	Kenosha
Johnson, Annette	Ogema	Wichman, Andy	Kenosha
Johnson, Marjorie	Viroqua	Wichman, Sandy	Kenosha
Jordan, Alex	Arena	Wichman, Eddy	Delavan
Keene, Shirley	Tomah	Wichman, Katy	Delavan
Knipping, Mark	Mineral Point	Wichman, Galvira	Kenosha
Knutson, Carole	West Salem	Wichman, Rebecca	Kenosha
Kruk, Janet	La Farge	Wynthein, Leslie	Arlington

OUR SPECIAL THANKS TO:

John Simpson and Tom Meinhover for their enthusiasm and support.
Wendy Penta and Tim Miller for their assistance.

Drawings from:
Red Mill Colonial Shop — Covered Bridge
Cupola House
Frank Lloyd Wright Warehouse
House on the Rock

Recipe reprints:
"Fry Bread" — *The Flavor of Wisconsin: An Informal History of Food and Eating in the Badger State*, Harva Hachten (State Historical Society of Wisconsin)
"Stone Soup" — *Kickapoo Pearls*

Song:
"Jam at Gerry's Rock"

Poem:
"Four Lakes of Madison", Henry Wadsworth Longfellow

Organizations that contributed information:
Cheese Makers Association
Green Bay Packers
International Institute of Milwaukee County
Kickapoo Valley Association
Milwaukee Brewers
Packer Hall of Fame
Pendarvis
State Historical Society of Wisconsin
Summerfest

The following sources:
Complete Works of Longfellow
Discovering Wisconsin, Polly Brody
Travel Guide to Historical Markers, Nancy Hochstetter
Wisconsin, August Derleth
Wisconsin, A History, R.N. Current
Wisconsin Folklore, Walker Wyman
Wisconsin Lore, Robert Gard and L.G. Sorden
"Wisconsin Trails", magazine
Wisconsin, Writer's Program

Additional Copies of "Recipes From Wisconsin...With Love"
can be ordered for $8.50, plus $1.00 for postage and handling
from:

New Boundary Designs Inc.
1453 Park Road
Chanhassen, MN 55317

Make checks payable to
New Boundary Designs Inc.